Portrait
OF PASSION

Portrait
OF PASSION

Written by Gail B. Stewart

Photographed by Paul H. Phillips

Foreword by Julie Foudy

COMPETITIVE IMAGE
PUBLISHING

foreword

When I think of the U.S. Women's Soccer Team past and present, I always find myself smiling. Various faces, players and staff have come and gone in the twenty-plus years since the team's inception. But regardless of whether it was the very first World Cup in 1991 or the most recent in 2007, there has been an ever-present energy and love of the game that makes the title of this book perfectly fitting.

This team is, and always has been, full of passion. Passion for the game, passion for each other, and passion for the fans. It is what motivated us. It is what kept me playing for the National Team for almost two decades.

As a member of this team—and I know it hasn't changed since I left—everywhere we went, laughter followed. It was contagious and we wanted to share it with the world. We hoped young girls would watch and think, "Ahhhh, **they** are **me**." We wanted girls to realize that big dreams are courageous, not crazy. We wanted girls to see that truly believing in that dream would make obstacles seem not insurmountable challenges, but rather like mere blips.

The players then and now have this wonderful ability to take themselves very seriously when it comes to preparation before games. But when practice is complete, when the game is over, the players also know that taking themselves too seriously is thankfully discouraged. A fine balance indeed.

You will see it in the beautiful portraits in this book—the grins, the grimaces, the joy, the determination, the strength, and at times, the pain. You will hear it in their personal stories, too—the reasons they began playing, the heroes whom they emulated, the frustrations through which they battled to become the great players they are today.

When people see the women's national team, they often only see the final product—the team standing on a podium accepting a medal. The beauty of this team is also in the quiet moments when no one is watching. The beauty of this team is in the long conversations in hotel hallways, when no one else can hear them. The beauty of this team is on the bus where dreams are shared. The beauty of this team is in the journey that few get to glimpse inside.

This book will give you that rare glimpse and reveal the personalities that spill over. Throughout it all, you will feel their passion and hear their laughter, because it is what defines this team.

As E.E. Cummings so wisely once said: "The most wasted of all days is one without laughter." And, I would add, one without passion. With that said, I hope you enjoy the wonderful images and stories about these amazing athletes.

Julie Foudy
#11 USA

Julie Foudy

National Hall of Fame inductee 2007
Former Captain U.S. Women's Soccer Team
Olympic Gold Medalist 1996, 2004
Olympic Silver Medalist 2000
Two-time World Cup Champion 1991, 1999
17-year veteran of National Team

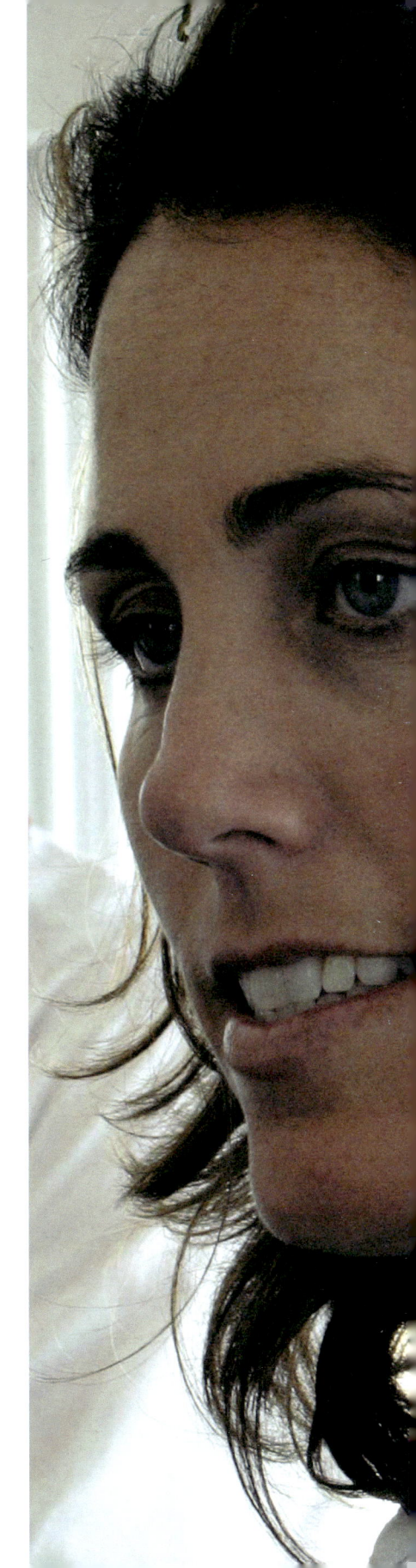

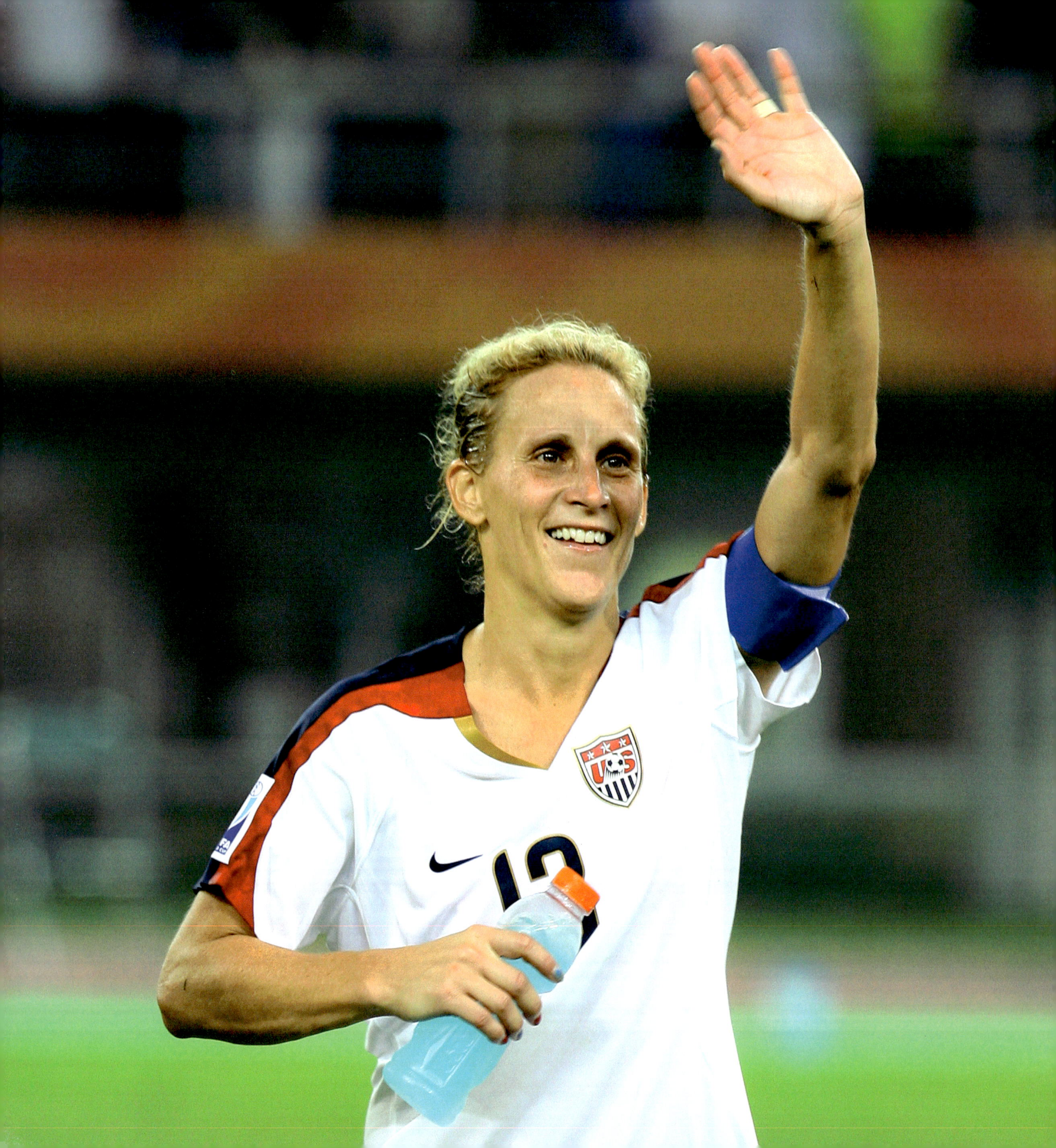

players

2007 WNT roster

Goalkeepers
- 1 Briana Scurry—Dayton, MN; UMass
- 18 Hope Solo—Richland, WA; Washington
- 21 Nicole Barnhart—Gilbertsville, PA; Stanford

Defenders
- 2 Marian Dalmy—Lakewood, CO; Santa Clara
- 3 Christie Rampone—Point Pleasant, NJ; Monmouth
- 4 Cat Whitehill—Birmingham, AL; UNC
- 8 Tina Ellertson—Vancouver, WA; Washington
- 14 Stephanie (Lopez) Cox —Elk Grove, CA; Portland
- 15 Kate Markgraf—Bloomfield Hills, MI; Notre Dame

Midfielders
- 7 Shannon Boxx—Redondo Beach, CA; Notre Dame
- 10 Aly Wagner—San Jose, CA; Santa Clara
- 11 Carli Lloyd—Delran, NJ; Rutgers
- 12 Leslie Osborne—Brookfield, WI; Santa Clara
- 16 Angela Hucles—Virginia Beach, VA; Virginia
- 17 Lori Chalupny—St. Louis, MO; UNC
- 19 Marci (Jobson) Miller—St. Charles, IL; SMU

Forwards
- 5 Lindsay Tarpley—Kalamazoo, MI; UNC
- 6 Natasha Kai—Kahuku, HI; Hawaii
- 9 Heather O'Reilly—East Brunswick, NJ; UNC
- 13 Kristine Lilly—Wilton, CT; UNC
- 20 Abby Wambach—Rochester, NY; Florida

Heather O'Reilly, Cat Whitehill and Lilly

Captain, Kristine Lilly

Natasha Kai

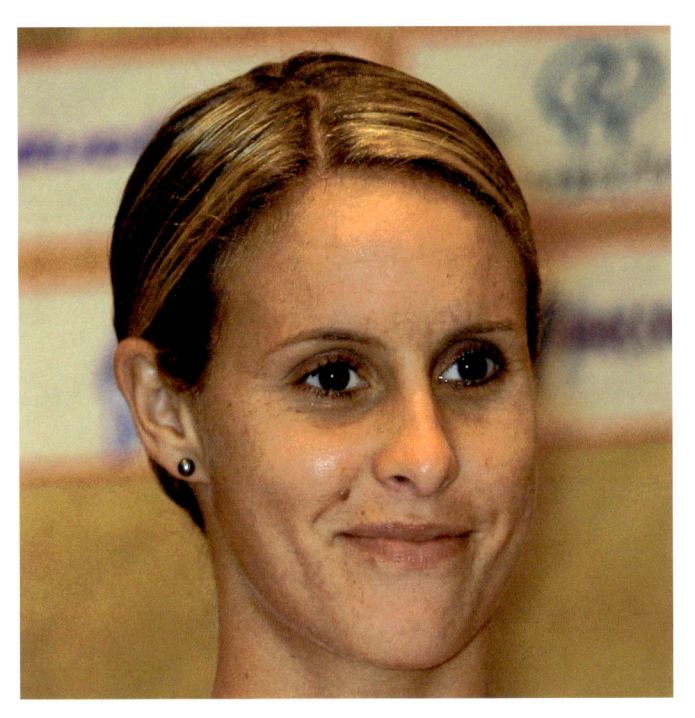

Leslie Osborne

Cat Whitehill

Heather O'Reilly

Abby Wambach

Lindsay Tarpley   Carli Lloyd

Shannon Boxx   Christie Rampone

Lori Chalupny   Hope Solo

Aly Wagner

Angela Hucles

Marci (Jobson) Miller

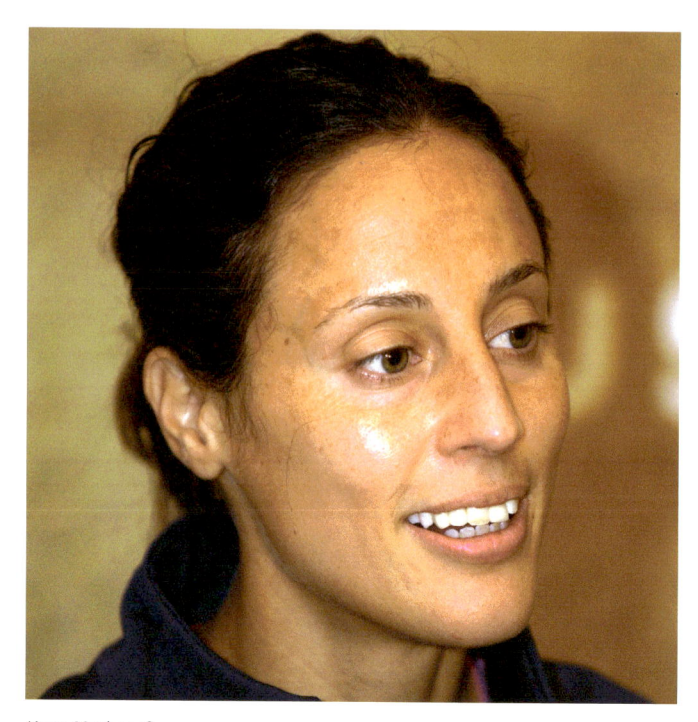

Kate Markgraf

Stephanie (Lopez) Cox

Nicole Barnhart

Marian Dalmy

Briana Scurry

Tina Ellertson

16

preface

This is a look at twenty-one women who are not at all alike, but at the same time have everything in common. I interviewed each of them in depth, learning about what life is like at the highest level of women's soccer. In the process I learned why millions of young soccer players throughout the United States are so energized by them, why so many fans of the game hold them in such esteem.

I found out what they were like as little kids, and what their families were like. I learned how they got addicted to soccer and what was the hardest part of the game to learn. I found out when they realized they actually had a chance to get to this level, and what it was like to be on the road in China for the World Cup. I learned who's got superstitions to get them through the toughest games. I learned, too, what they would change if they could go back to being a twelve-year-old soccer player—and their answers may surprise you.

The stories of the women are illustrated by the photographs of Paul Phillips, who followed the team from Chicago to China as they prepared for and competed in the World Cup. In addition to the exciting game images, Paul captured lots of candid off-the-field shots.

The result, I think, is a portrait of a team of passionate, highly talented athletes. It offers a glimpse of why the U.S. Women's Team has achieved so much, and why today's young soccer players might find inspiration in their stories.

—Gail B. Stewart

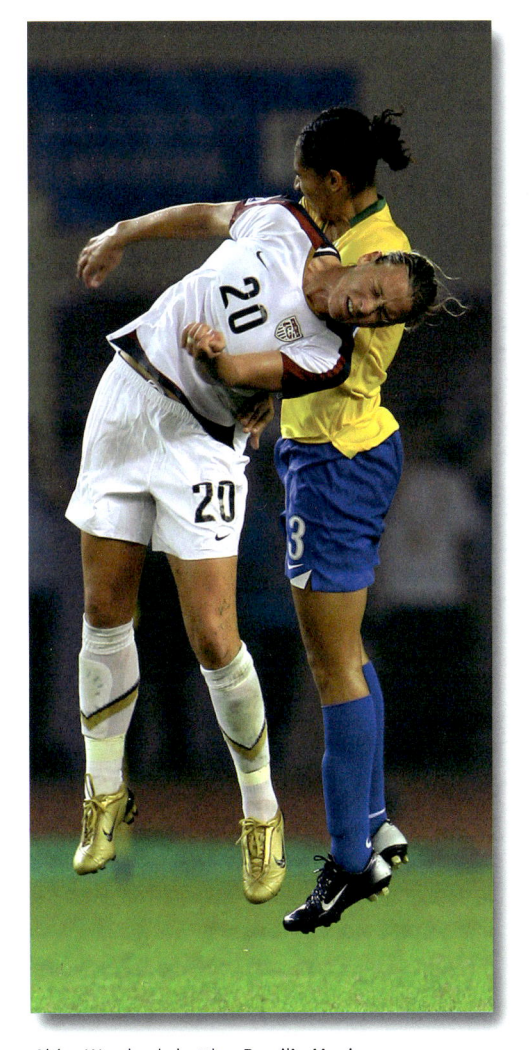

Abby Wambach battles Brazil's Monica.

Clockwise from top left:
Lori Chalupny, Heather O'Reilly, Kristine Lilly, Angela Hucles

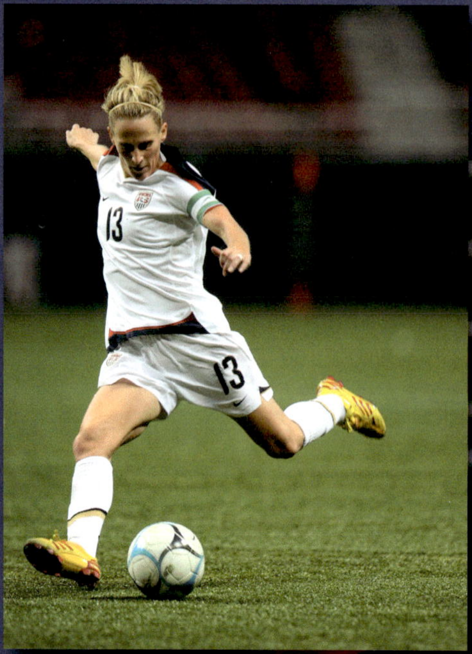

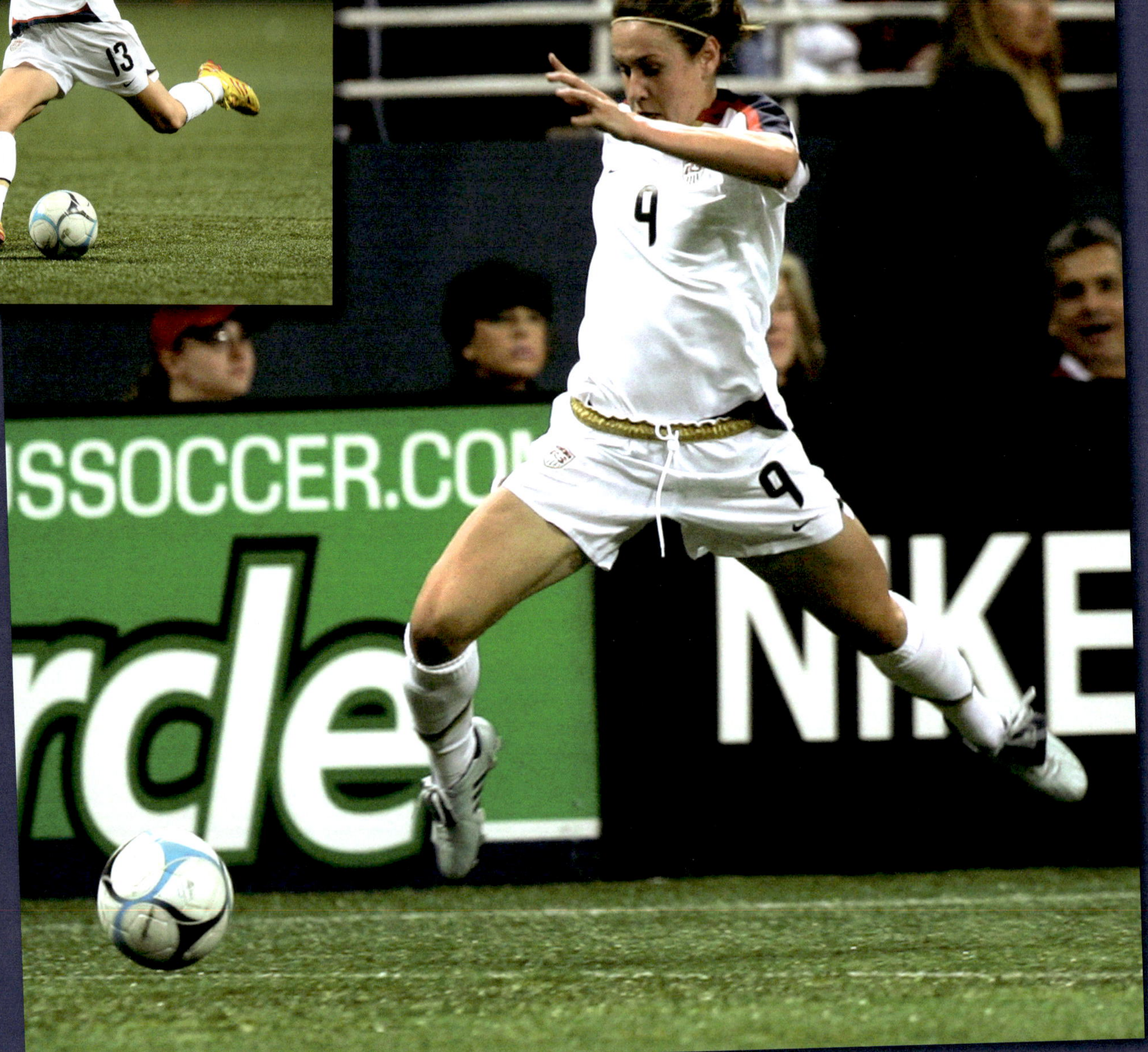
NIKE

chapter 1

Christie Rampone, age 2

first kicks

Anyone who thinks that there is a "typical" background of a U.S. National team member has not met this group of young women. They come from cities, suburbs, and little towns. They are from places as diverse as Hawaii and New Jersey, and just about everywhere in between. Some were members of country clubs, and others had parents struggling just to make ends meet. But while their family backgrounds differ widely, they all have one thing in common: Every member of the team credits her family for her early interest in athletics.

"It's My Parents"

Cat Whitehill, a proud native of Birmingham, Alabama, says her father was determined that his daughters learn how to throw and catch a ball correctly. "So my dad and my sister and I spent a lot of time playing football in the backyard," she says. "Those are some of my best memories growing up. I still passionately love football."

For Marian Dalmy's parents, getting their daughter into sports seemed a necessity. "I was always running," says Dalmy. "Lots—seriously, lots—of energy. I kept my parents running around, literally. When they would go play tennis, I'd spend the entire time climbing around on the fence. It was probably a relief for them when I started playing soccer, so I had something more constructive to do with all that energy."

Nicole Barnhart, age 6

What Was Your First Team?

With all the soccer memories the women have accumulated over the years—awards, championship matches, even the Olympic games—it is amazing how many of them can remember their very first team.

Kristine Lilly
I have no idea what the team was called or what we wore. But I do have vivid memories of those orange slices at half time.

Marci Miller
I have no idea what the name was, or what color we wore. But I can tell you that when we won, our coach Mr. Lyten would take us to the Dairy Queen for blizzards. That is a great memory!

Kate Markgraf
I was on the Green Wave. And we had very cool mesh green and white shirts.

Abby Wambach
Let's see—I was on the Stars. And we wore maroon shirts.

Cat Whitehill
I was on the Wildcats back in Alabama. Blue and white shirts for us.

> "We were the Sparklers. We had pink shirts and black shorts. Very cute."
> Marian Dalmy

For some of the women, brothers or sisters were their motivation for beginning sports. "My sister Gillian is four years older than me," says Shannon Boxx. "I spent a lot of time with her taking care of me. I also spent a lot of time really idolizing her. She was everything I wanted to be.

"My mom is a single mom, and she depended on my sister to help keep track of me. And Gillian was on baseball and soccer teams when I was little. I begged my mom to let me play, too. That's all I wanted to do. I'm not sure if the motivation was actually playing the sport, or just so I could be like Gillian."

Angela Hucles, age 9

"You Either Sink or Swim"

In some cases, it was a player's role within her family that helped create a competitive spirit. Lindsay Tarpley credits her older brother with teaching her to be aggressive, even as a little girl. "I spent a lot of time with him, trying to figure out how to do what he was doing," she recalls. "He really pushed me to my limits, challenging me, playing sports with me. He'd mark me in pickup games—he really didn't go easy on me because he was bigger and stronger than I was. He never let me win—at least not that I remember. I do remember being frustrated and crying when I couldn't beat him. He was tough on me, but it made me work harder. And," she says, "he could pick on me, but none of his friends could."

Kristine Lilly, age 11

Sometimes it was the sheer number of children in a family that created a competitive spirit. "I was the youngest of seven kids," says Abby Wambach. "That can toughen you up. I think I was always confident—I had to be as the youngest in my family. You had to believe in yourself, or you'd get lost in the

Heather O'Reilly age 12

Aly Wagner still practices her juggling.

mix. You had to either sink or swim. For me, swimming was the only option."

Marci Miller couldn't agree more. She grew up in a large family, too, as the youngest of eight. "It was a very competitive family," she says. "I mean, we'd compete hard for everything—from backyard games, video games—even for our parents' attention. With all those kids—it forced me to keep up. I had to. It's just how you survive in a big active family. So getting psyched up for a soccer game, getting that competitive spirit going—that has never been hard for me."

She also says that growing up in a big family made it easier for her to take criticism. She did not fall apart when criticized by soccer coaches. "The thing is, you'll always get criticism, but you just have to keep doing your best. That's one thing I learned in my big family—you've got to let things roll off your back, don't focus on the bad things. Just keep working hard. I don't know that I would have been able to do that without the family I have."

"The World Does Not Revolve Around Me"

Some team members insist that while they got lots of support from their families when they showed early signs of athleticism, they received some even more valuable lessons, too. These lessons have helped them become players who are kinder, more generous, and more team-oriented.

Stephanie Lopez is a good example. She has three biological brothers, as well as three foster siblings. "My parents were foster parents," she says, "and I had two sisters and another brother who lived with us from when I was in first grade to sophomore year of high school. I shared a room with my foster sisters, and we were close. Our whole family was close."

" 1500 times "

"When I was nine," says Aly Wagner, "my soccer coach told me that by the time he was ten, he could do one hundred juggles. I worked hard and did that, too. That was my goal. But then I set a higher one. By the time I was ten, I could juggle 1500 times."

As a youth, Wagner's juggling skills helped her control the ball during games.

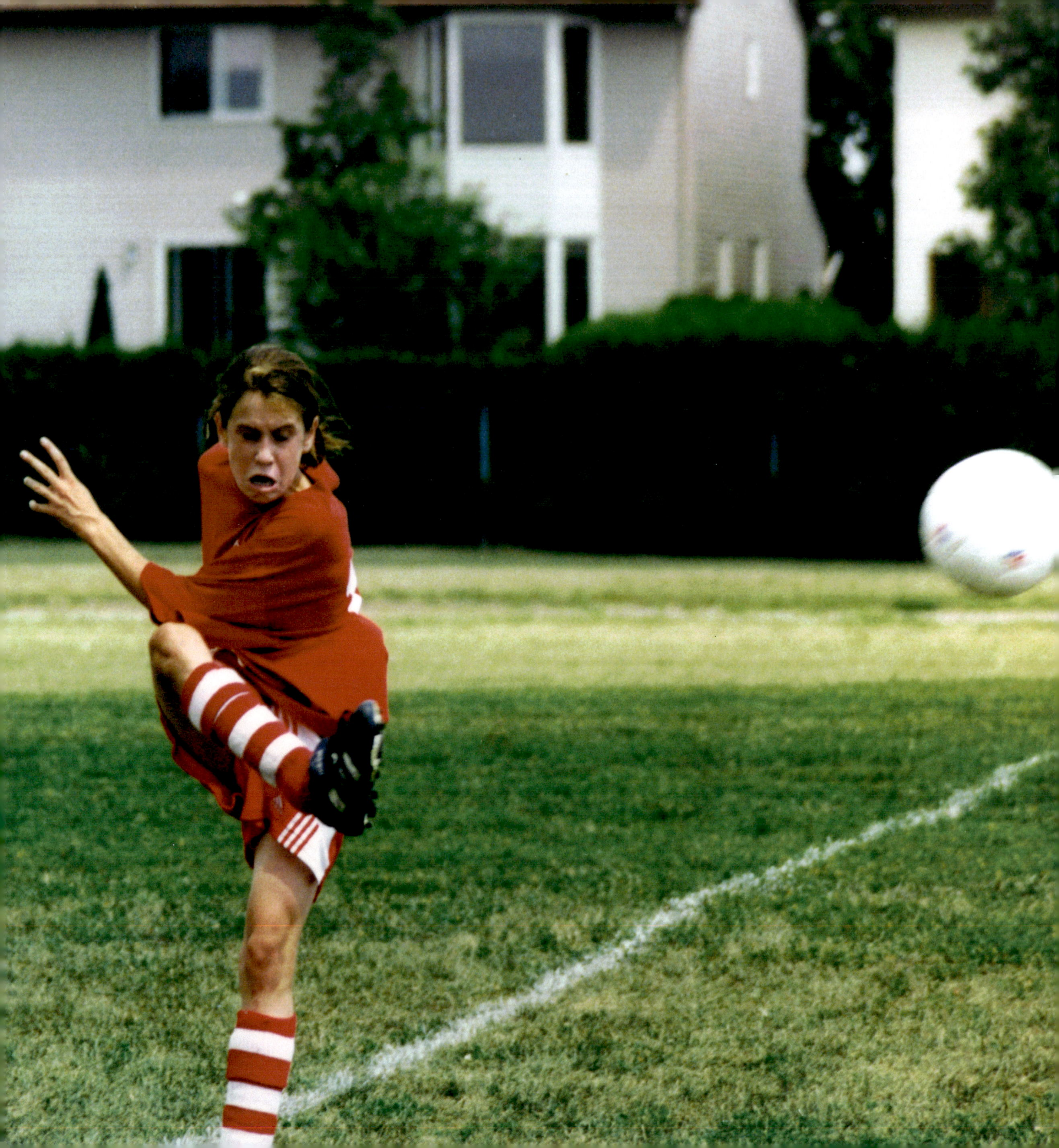

She says that her family was a constant source of stability—something for which she has been grateful ever since. "It's kind of hard to explain," she says. "It was a sense of being down to earth, of being real. My parents didn't highlight one person's successes over another person. They kept me focused, and that was good. They taught me not to brag, but rather be aware of other people. I learned that with our family. I didn't have to be reminded that there were kids with fewer advantages—I was living with three of them. They had more challenges, more troubles in their lives than I had.

"Anyway, I think that helped me keep my priorities right—and I am so grateful for that every time I play a game. The world does not revolve around me, and that's how it should be. It keeps me grounded, makes me aware of other people's feelings. Even now—I'm proud to be on this team, representing my country. But treating my teammates the right way—that, to me, is as important as our record."

"I Loved Diagramming Sentences"

For some of them, their early prowess in sports was matched with good grades in school. Tina Ellertson's parents were both African immigrants—her mother from Nigeria and her father from Ghana. "They came to the United States when they were twenty-one years old," she says. "They got scholarships and came here to study. And they really stressed education to us kids."

She ended high school with a 3.7 grade point average, and credits her parents for that achievement. "They came here on a dream," she says simply. "For them, an education was everything. America is the land of opportunity, and without a good education, it's hard to make a difference."

O'Reilly reacts in a game against Mexico.

Heather O'Reilly played on a Summer Select team in Canada when she was 13.

Angela Hucles competed on a boy's team as a 12-year-old.

Midfielder Andrea Hucles says her grades were not that impressive, but says she did enjoy school. "My favorite was English—especially grammar. I know that sounds very odd, but it's true. We had a teacher in fourth grade who taught us how to diagram sentences. I loved diagramming sentences. We were doing eighth grade work in fourth grade—it was great. I loved that. Not everything about school, but that part was really great."

"I Was the Kid Who Brought Every Single Book Home"

Christie Rampone shakes her head. "I'm not like those guys," she says. "I wasn't good in school. It didn't come easy to me, like sports did—which was frustrating. I was the kid who brought every single book home every night in my backpack. I studied hard all night. I didn't enjoy it—but I was competitive, you know? I wanted to excel. So I tried hard. But it was always a struggle for me. My sister used to make fun of me. I'd get up at five in the morning, just to have extra preparation time. I had the discipline, but not the ability, I guess."

Hucles goes for a header against Mexico.

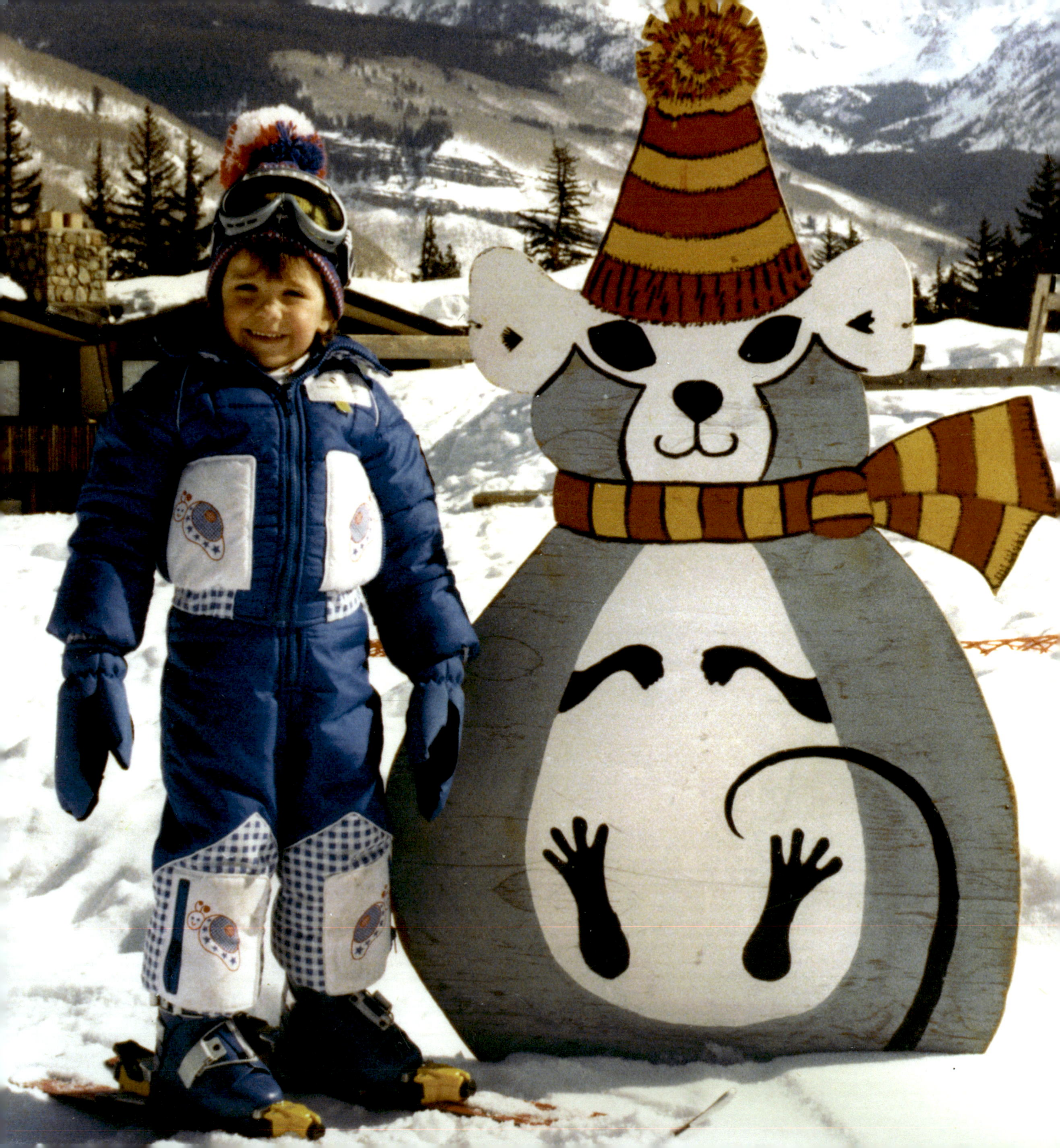

She says that it is important not to minimize that discipline, however. "I mean, even without that natural ability, you can achieve a lot by working really hard. Even in college, I'd take every paper I wrote to the writing lab. They have people working there who will go over papers, check them over, make suggestions. I took advantage of that help, though a lot of people don't. Maybe they don't need to, I don't know. And I never had tutors, but I took advantage of teachers who had office hours. I'd go in for extra help. Like I said, it was more work, but it got me through."

Natasha Kai, who grew up in Hawaii, admits that school and studying were never strong suits for her. "I was the class clown," she admits. "My parents stressed school, and I did try. I tried to be serious, because I know it's important. But I was always interested more in soccer. Let's say that in school I just got by."

She says that one huge challenge to her sixth grade education was that her mother was her spelling teacher. "I had a hard time not calling her Mom instead of Mrs. Kai," she says. "And when I did forget, all the other kids would call her Mom, too, just to be funny."

That year, she had done very well in most of her subjects. "In fact," she says, "I almost had straight A's. I even had an A in math, which I hated. But my mom had given me a C in spelling. I thought it was a joke, but it wasn't. She told me, 'You're my daughter, but you're one of my students. In class you're a student. You're not good in spelling, so I gave you a C.'"

More than ten years later, Kai still sounds baffled at her mother's reasoning. "I was like, wow," she says.

Wagner with Nicole Barnhart peeking over her shoulder

Aly Wagner was into skiing at a young age.

Lori Chalupny, age 13

"Who Wants a Girlfriend Who Could Beat Them Up?"

None recall that soccer was their only sport, or even their favorite—at least when they were little girls. "In my neighborhood you played everything," says Shannon Boxx. "For me, besides soccer, I ended up playing baseball, basketball, ice hockey. And when I got older, I played flag football with the boys in middle school. I was a total tomboy—good in sports, short hair. But I remember wearing earrings so people knew I was a girl."

Carli Lloyd agrees that playing sports meant spending more time with boys. "I played all the sports, too—softball, basketball, whatever. And yeah, I was stereotyped as a tomboy. It was kind of big thing back then. I got teased. But the thing is, the older I got, the cooler it got to be—playing sports. So it ended up okay."

Heather O'Reilly says that her three older brothers encouraged her to be an athlete for personal reasons. "They always let me play because sometimes I could show up their friends," she says. "And they found that really amusing. So running with the boys was just what I did, I guess. I will say that as I got older, some of the boys got intimidated because I was so sporty. I mean, who wants a girlfriend who could beat them up? I was still proud of being good in sports, but sometimes it was uncomfortable."

Cat Whitehill says that when she started soccer, it wasn't that she didn't want to play with other girls—it wasn't a choice. "There weren't that many girls playing who were that competitive. And in lots of places, like my hometown, there weren't the same opportunities for girls as for boys. No all-girl teams. So I played on boys' teams up through eighth grade. I never had the mentality to let the boys win, or worry about that stuff. I just wanted to win—I was competitive."

What Does MVP Mean?

Heather O'Reilly says that from the beginning, soccer was something she excelled at, although laughs that she didn't always understand the awards she received.

"I remember sitting in the car on the ride home from an end of the season banquet. I'd gotten the MVP award, and I didn't understand what it meant. I asked, 'What does MVP mean?' I was six or seven, I think. Then my brother said it meant 'Most Valuable Player.' I still didn't get it. He finally just said, 'It means you're the best player.'"

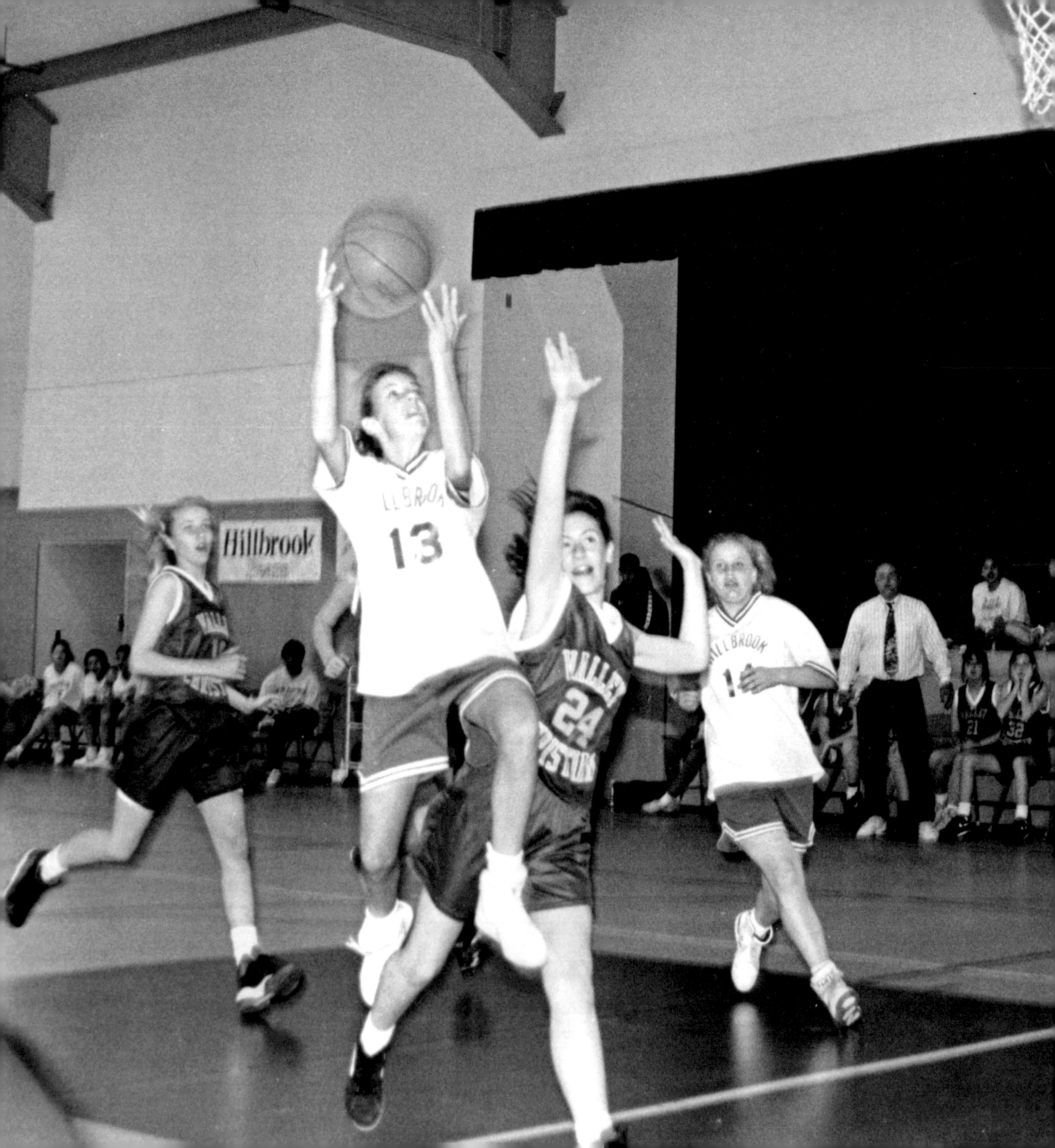
Hillbrook
13
HILLBROOK
24

Looking for Role Models

Most team members say that as young girls, they had idols—people whom they respected and tried to emulate as they grew up. Interestingly, however, not all of their idols were soccer players. In fact, for many of the older members of the team, women soccer players were nonexistent when they were growing up. Team leader Kristine Lilly says that when she was a little girl, soccer in general was ignored by the American media—even more so than it is today.

"I knew about Pelé," she says. "He was absolutely great. But for soccer role models, he was pretty much it. And even as amazing as he was, soccer didn't get on television much at all. I did like watching other women athletes—especially during the Olympics. Nadia Comaneci, the gymnast from Romania, was fun to watch on television. I guess back then, I didn't really think about being what kind of athlete I wanted to be. I just wanted to grow up to be someone who could do amazing things in some sport."

Goalkeeper Briana Scurry says that she had much the same experience growing up. "I grew up loving basketball as much as soccer, if not more so. So I followed the college career of Cheryl Miller at USC. And Pearl Washington, another basketball great. The two of them demonstrated that there could be a future for someone like me in sports. They were strong young women, and they were great role models. That was a huge incentive for me."

Abby Wambach laughs about her own idols. "They were Kristine [Lilly] and Mia Hamm, Julie Foudy," she says. "They were the greats. They paved the way for people like me. I had autographs, posters in my room, I was surrounded by their images when I was growing up. I wanted to be them. I guess to me it

Carli Lloyd is still a Phillies fan.

Aly Wagner played basketball for the Hillbrook Bears in Los Gatos, California.

" we were like *The Simpsons* "

Goalkeeper Hope Solo grew up in the town of Richland, Washington. The town is famous for building the atomic bomb that ended World War II.

"We were like *The Simpsons*," she says. "You know how everybody in that town works at the nuclear power plant? That was what it was like in Richland. And the teams from Richland were always strong. People used to joke that the reason for our good athletes was some genetic thing that happened because of a nuclear accident at the plant."

is that much more amazing that these players accomplished so much without having any female soccer role models themselves. It makes their accomplishments seem even greater."

Early Clues

Asked if their performance on their first teams showed any indication of future ability, the team members have mixed reactions. Kristine Lilly says she doesn't think anyone was impressed with her ability early on. "I have pictures

Carli Lloyd learning the basics at age 6

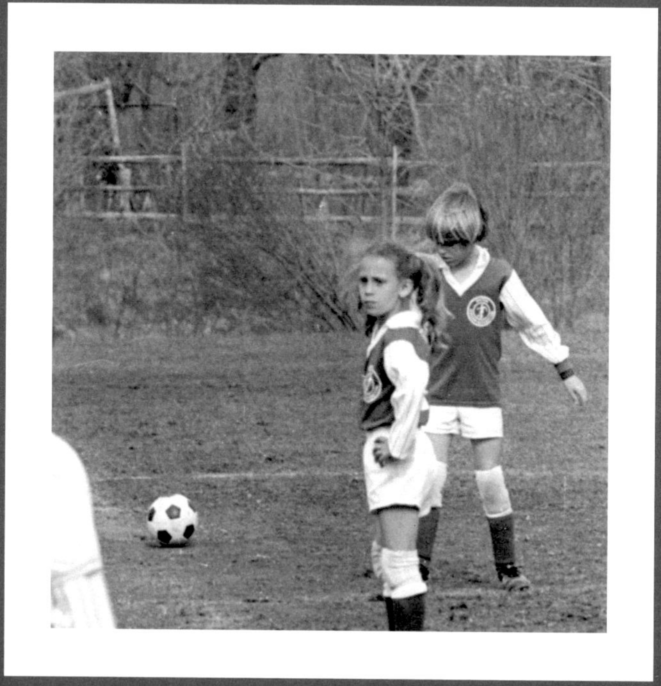

of me just sort of standing there," she says. "I think I was waiting for the ball to come to me, not doing much of anything. Maybe by age ten or eleven things picked up a little."

Not so for Aly Wagner. She says something just clicked right away when she first started playing. "I was an attacking player even as a kid," she says. "Lots of dribbling. I scored a lot of goals, even when I was little. At school, during recess, I'd go up on the field and play with the boys. I'd be the only girl, but it was much more fun."

Sometimes, she says, she would feel a little shy being the only girl with all those boys. "Once in awhile," she says, " I'd tried to convince another girl to go up there with me and play, but that was usually pretty hard to do."

For Natasha Kai, whether she was good at the game was not even an issue. For her, she says, soccer meant freedom—if only for an hour or two each week. "For me it was a way to not have to babysit for my younger brothers and sisters all the time," she admits. "I mean, I didn't really mind—I love my family. But you know, everybody needs some time to themselves. So anyway, when some friends started playing on a soccer team—I was seven, I think—I thought I should maybe do that, too. It wasn't about soccer. It was just a way to do something with my friends. And not babysit. That was the important part."

Later, she says, she would realize that soccer could be important for other reasons, too.

Kristine Lilly, age 8

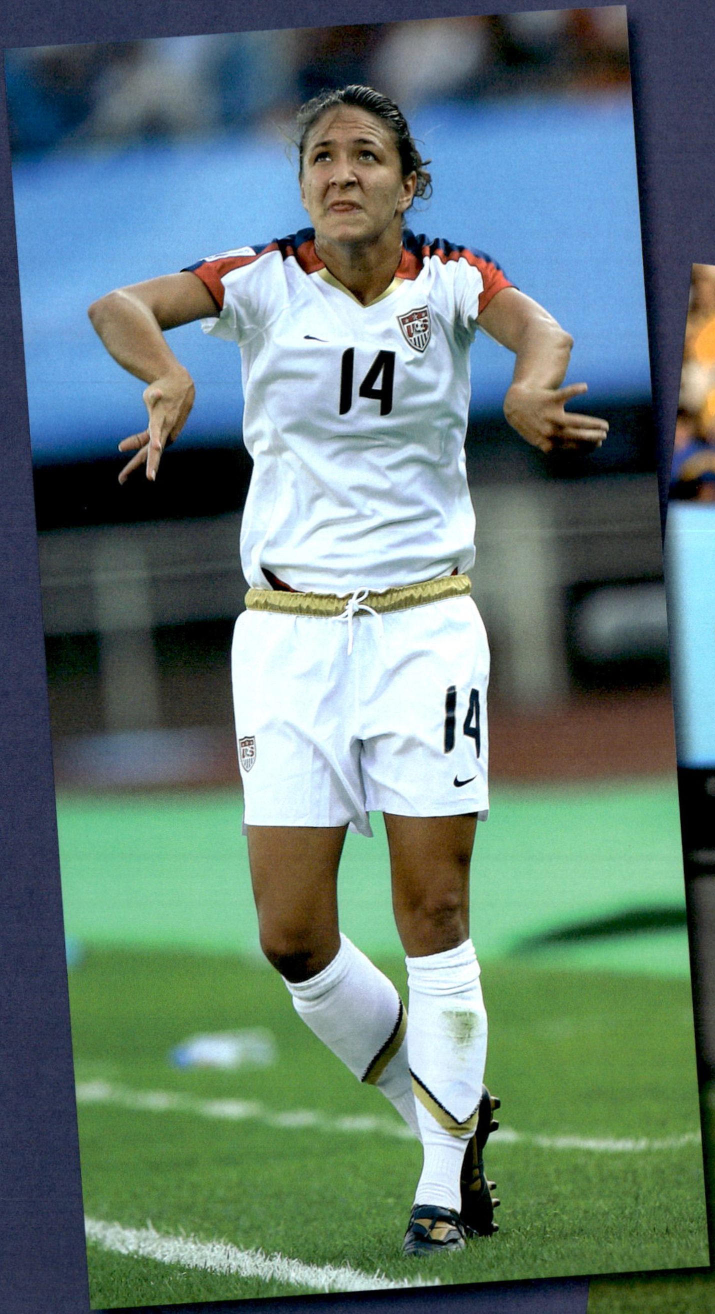

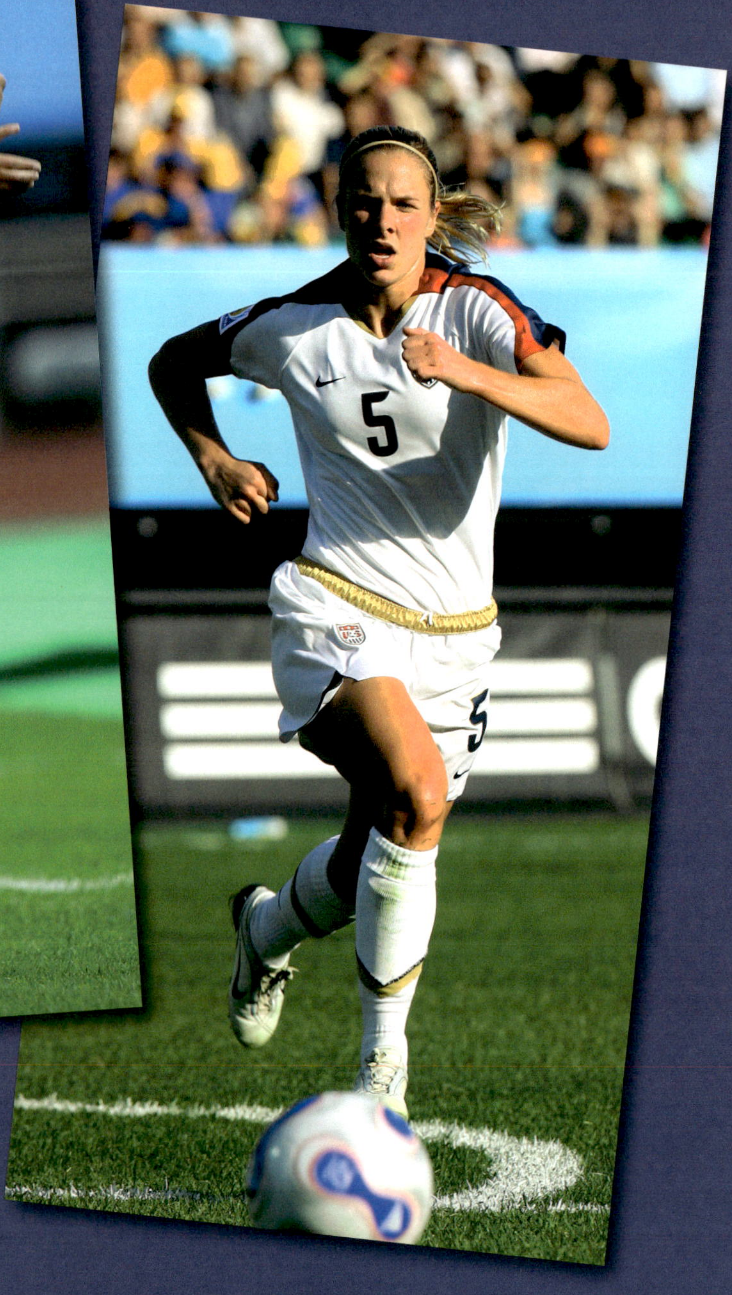

chapter 2

Christie Rampone was 8 when she raced on "Field Day" at Ocean Road Elementary in Point Pleasant, New Jersey.

getting game

There are difficult jumps to be made between being a recreational soccer player and becoming a serious, skilled player. As the girls got older, they found that soccer had begun to feel more important. Even though they might have been playing lots of different sports, somewhere along the line, somehow soccer had begun to feel more important than the others.

For some of the girls, soccer's growing prominence was due to the support and urging of a coach who saw glimmers of possibilities in how she handled the ball. In other cases, it was simply that she found herself looking forward to a Saturday morning soccer game more than a swim meet or a softball tournament. Either way, soccer had taken a place of honor in her world.

"Pick One"

Goalkeeper Nicole Barnhart was surprised by the enthusiastic support of people around her. "I played a lot of sports—lacrosse, basketball, baseball, soccer," she says. "And where I grew up in Pennsylvania had no girls' teams, so all the way through high school I played with the boys. And I must have gotten better because of competing with them, I guess. I didn't recognize that I was good in soccer. It took other people—coaches, other players—telling me I had talent. Really, it was fun for me, but I never even considered that I could go further with soccer—not until then."

Rampone brings a lot of intensity to each game.

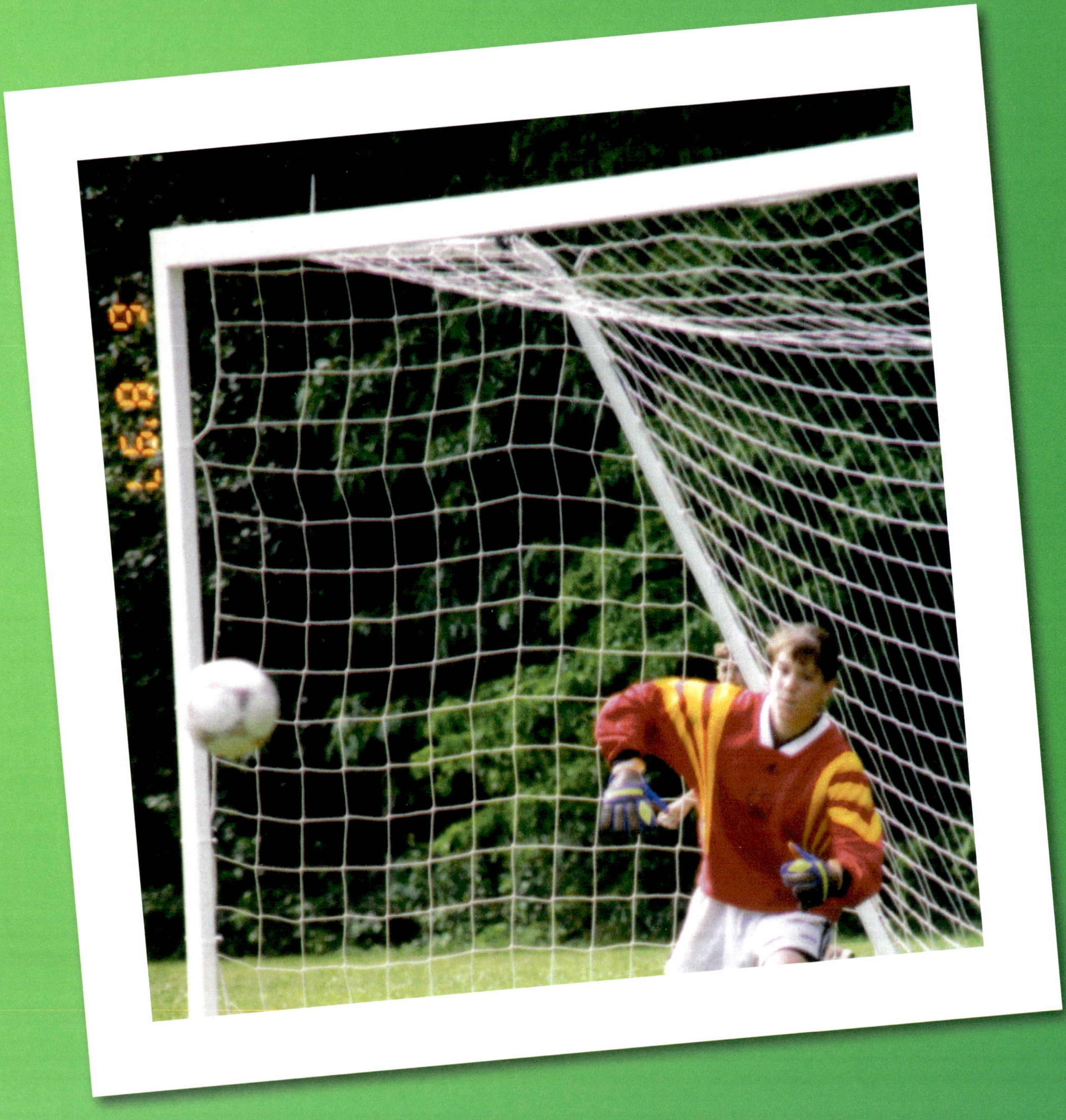

Leslie Osborne laughs about how she got her start as a serious player. She never actually made a decision to concentrate on soccer. In fact, no one made that decision. It was, quite literally, the luck of the draw. "I was thirteen," she says, "and my dad sat me down and told me that I was doing too much running around with too many sports. I mean, I had done swimming, gymnastics, basketball, running, tennis—I'd done almost every sport. But it was getting really crazy for my parents having to drive to all these meets and tournaments and practices. So he told me to get a hat. I wrote down each of the sports on a piece of paper and he made me pick one that I would concentrate on from the hat. And the paper I picked was soccer."

Osborne says that at the time, neither she nor her parents had any idea of the significance of that pick. "Really, if I'd drawn something else, maybe tennis or something would have been my sport. They actually thought I was better in tennis than soccer. But anyway, that's how it turned out!"

More Than One Road

Once each of these girls felt that soccer was her sport, it was important to see how far she could go with it. The ultimate goal, of course, was making the National Team—the team that would represent the United States in the Olympics or the World Cup. There is a structure in place for young soccer players to get evaluated by high-level trainers. The trainers could determine whether the players had the talent to compete at the highest levels.

One very visible structure for spotlighting the best young players was, and remains, the Olympic Development Program, or ODP. Tryouts for ODP teams

Barnhart is happy to be on the WNT as the third goalkeeper.

Nicole Barnhart was an ODP player.

Leslie Osborne chose soccer over swimming, gymnastics, basketball, running and tennis.

are held throughout the country, and presumed to draw the most talented players. Many of the current National Team members made their ODP teams, and found themselves competing for regional teams, and even national youth teams. In many cases, the system works. But not always. There are many, many highly talented players who, for one reason or another, do not take the ODP route. And some have even ended up on the National Team.

"I'm an example of one of those kids that didn't do ODP," says Briana Scurry, smiling. "A lot of girls playing today think that if you don't make an ODP team, you have no future as a soccer player, but that's not right. I went to one regional tournament when I was thirteen, I think. And I didn't make the cut. They said I was athletic, but I needed polishing up. And one other time, one of my coaches sponsored me, I didn't make it then either. I was most improved, but wasn't chosen. And I couldn't afford to do ODP. That's an expensive thing, and my family couldn't spend that kind of money. So I just continued to play on my school team, and my club team."

"I was kind of the same," says Christie Rampone. "I didn't do the ODP, all that stuff for soccer. When I was in high school, basketball was my passion. I cut down on all the sports, but I kept two—basketball and soccer. I played soccer just for fun, but, as I say, basketball was my first love. Every camp or special training thing I did was for basketball, not soccer. And I went to college on a basketball scholarship. And it was lucky that at my college they let you play two sports. So I did soccer, too. I kind of fell in love with soccer in college—more than I ever had before."

"I Couldn't Even Order a Pizza"

One benefit Christie Rampone received from soccer was having a place where she wasn't shy. "I was always terribly shy," she says. "I couldn't talk on the phone. I couldn't even order a pizza, or talk to a friend about making a plan for the next day. Even in high school, when college coaches would call, I'd hate it."

"But somehow, when I'd walk onto the soccer field, I became a completely different person. I was more comfortable—just walking over the sideline! I'm not sure why. Maybe because I didn't have to talk much. All I had to do is show who I was by my actions."

"

" it wasn't the easiest system "

Teens who play on youth national teams are constantly having to find a balance between high school and traveling for matches. Cat Whitehill admits that like many of the players, she often found it a struggle trying to succeed on a highly competitive national team while still in high school.

"I loved school, up until I started doing all that traveling," she says. "Then it got hard. I was only in high school for weeks at a time, then I'd be gone for a couple of weeks. That all started sophomore year of high school for me. My teachers were all really understanding. They gave me all my assignments in advance, so I could do them on the road. But it isn't the same. It's hard to learn a language on your own, or math. It just wasn't the easiest system, at least for me."

Getting Serious

But no matter what path they chose toward their goal, they found that it was important to approach soccer in a different manner. For instance, many of them realized that the drills and practices they had done on their recreational or club teams were not going to be enough to help them be as well-prepared as they needed to be.

"For me it was learning what practice was all about," says Heather O'Reilly. "As I was growing up, I never really got it. I'd work on the stuff I was good at. I think it was because I always wanted to show off—I wanted to be the best. So that meant showing the coach what I was good at. So instead of working on my left foot, which I was not good at, I worked with my right foot. And that was time wasted."

O'Reilly says that now, when she coaches or does training sessions, she warns the girls not to make the same mistake she made. "I tell them, 'This is practice! If you don't do something very well, who cares! Work on what you are weakest at, not on your strengths.'"

Aly Wagner agrees. "I did the same exact thing when I'd practice. "I was always an attacking player, you know? I loved the dribbling, the shooting, the fun of getting around a defender. But as you get older, your coaches want you to practice other things, too, like individual defense—as in, what you'd do if the defender steals the ball.

"I didn't like working on that. I wanted to spend the least amount of time on it. To me, offense was fun—it was creative. But the concept of defense seemed like the opposite. Instead of creating something, you're breaking

Heather O'Reilly goes all out in practice.

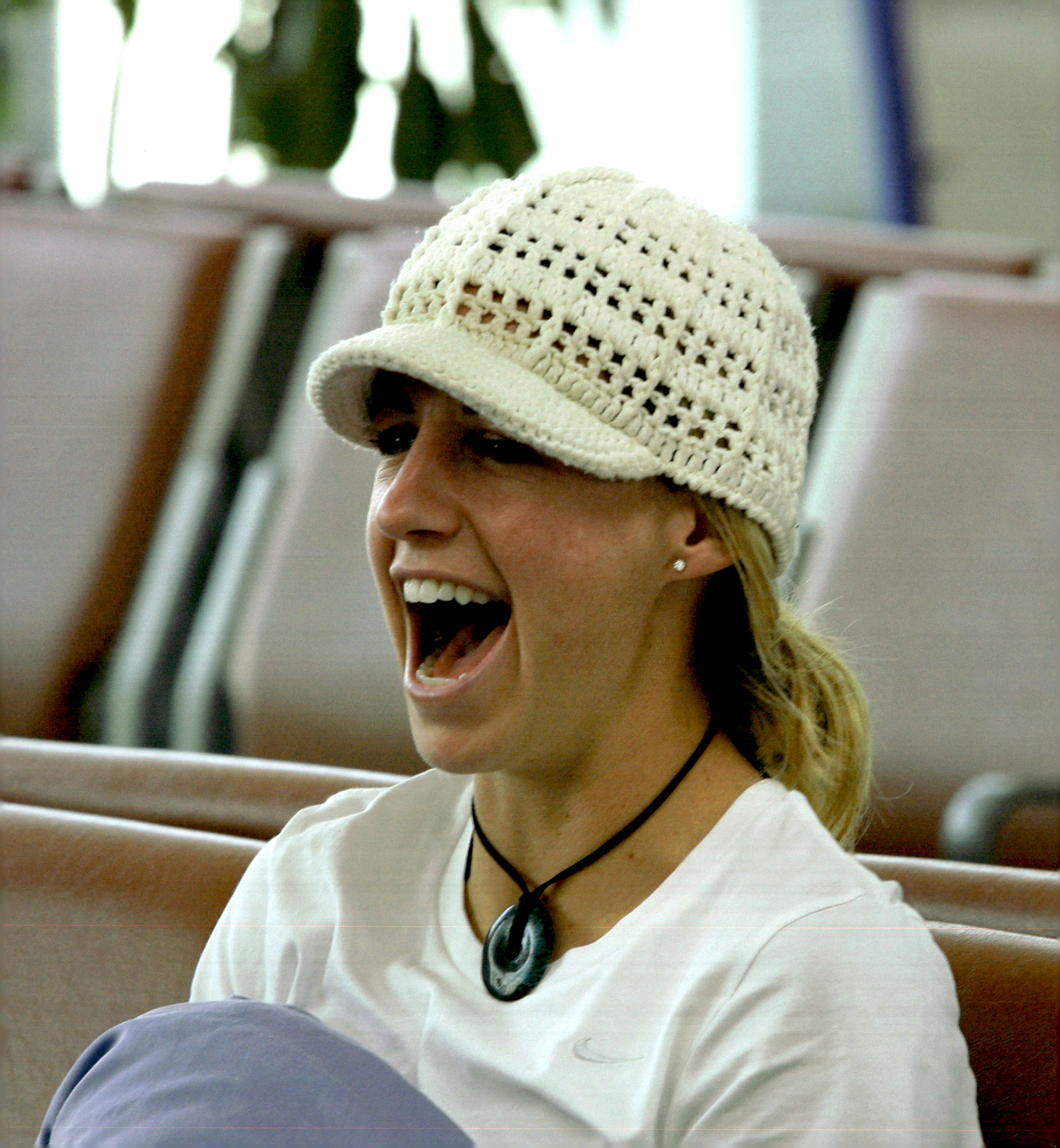

something up. Plus, if you really want to know the truth," she says, " when I did practice defense, if I got beat, I'd get mad. And that was no fun at all."

The Game in Your Head

Wagner says that was another aspect of the game she needed to work on as she got older—the psychological aspect. She needed to learn now to rein in her emotions when things weren't going her way. "I was a poor loser," she admits. "And it wasn't just soccer. Once when my sister beat me at ping pong, I broke the paddle, slammed it on the edge of the table so hard it split. Another time when she beat me at something, I kicked her door in. Yeah, bratty—you can say it."

She says that her emotions would really get the worst of her if she lost a soccer game. "It's learning that everything isn't about me," she says. "It's taken me until recently to realize that, to be able to make a mistake and quickly forget it. Otherwise, I'd be thinking about it, feeling bad until the next day. And again, that would be time wasted. I mean there's being competitive—which is a good thing—and there's going way overboard, forgetting that it's a team game. Nobody should take credit for winning. Nobody should take blame for losing. And I play much more confidently when I remember that."

Wagner's U18 team was coached by her mom.

Learning From Failing

Marian Dalmy has had the same experiences. "I was always comparing myself to other players. I bet a lot of younger players do that. I think it was pressure I was putting on myself. If people would compliment me, say I was

Aly Wagner has fun while waiting for a flight from Chengdu to Shanghai.

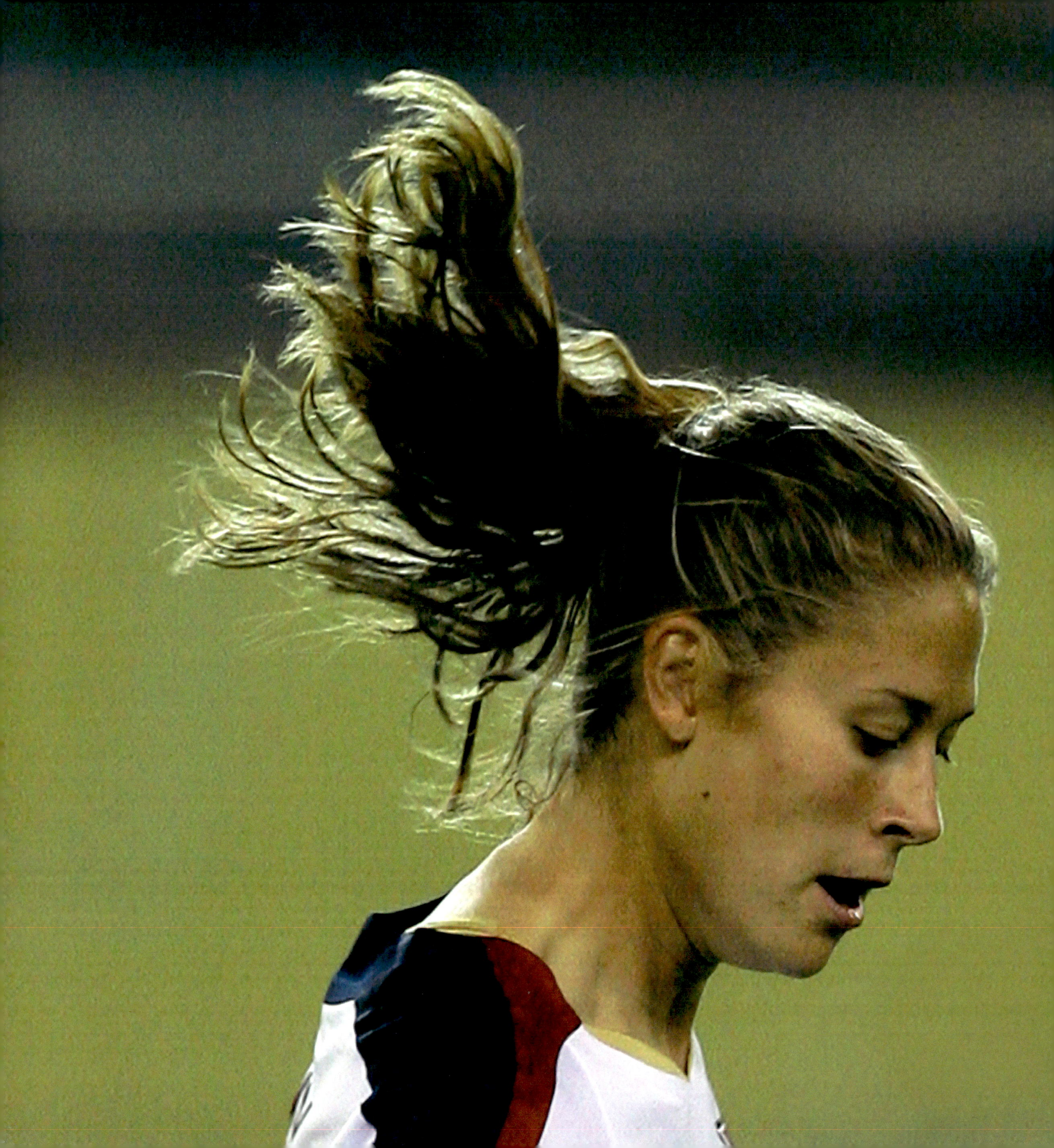

really good, I'd translate that into pressure to play better. And if I didn't play well, I'd beat myself up over it. If I didn't score a goal, I'd feel like I'd failed."

She has grown a lot in that aspect of her game, she says, because of having the experience of failing. "That sounds strange," she says, "but it's true. I remember in eighth or ninth grade, I was doing ODP. I was trying to make the state team, but almost got cut. The coach wasn't impressed by me. I got a chance, but was the last one picked for the team. That rattled me. I made the team, but it was just barely.

"Over the next few years, in high school, I guess I finally realized I couldn't depend on other people to build up my confidence. Otherwise, I'd be up and down, depending on whether this coach or that coach thought I was good or not. That's way too hard on you, you know? Look, you're always going to have coaches who don't help your confidence. They get on you for making mistakes. You can't let that destroy you emotionally. I think I've had to learn to find that strength from inside myself, not from other people. I can't control other people."

Dalmy says it has not been an easy lesson to learn, but the most valuable one. "I know now, that if I'm not playing well, if some part of my game isn't working, I can go back to doing basic things that I can rely on. Like if my shot isn't right, I can always make a good solid pass or a run, or something else that helps the team."

Marian Dalmy shows her concentration in World Cup match against Brazil.

"visible family ties"

When Natasha Kai compares her teammates to her family, it is the height of praise. She lives for her family, and that is physically obvious. "I've got seventeen tattoos," she says. "And most of them are about my family. I've got one that says 'Benny loves Sharon'—those are my parents. Oh, and I've got my last name with two turtles. In Hawaii, parents decide on an amakua for the family. That's like a guardian that protects us. And turtles are our amakua. And on the outside of my arms, I've got the names of all my siblings and my two nephews. Man, I spoil those guys!"

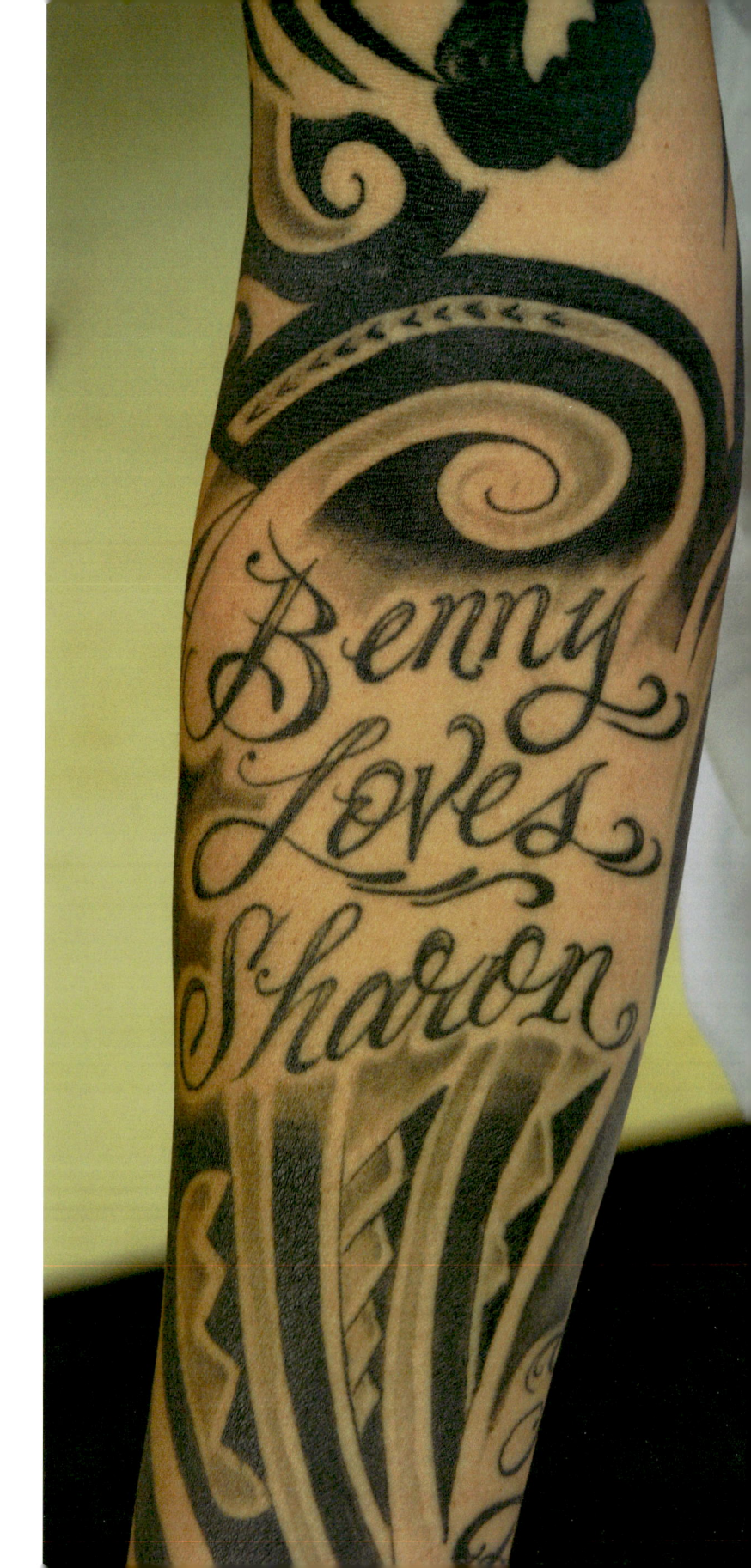

You Want Me to Play Where?

With some of the young women, growing as a player meant changing the position they play. This was especially true of goalies. Interestingly, few adult goalies say they started out in that position. Hope Solo started out as a field player. "Back then, goalie was the position you played if you couldn't dribble or kick," she says, laughing. "And when I was young, I was really good in the field. It actually wasn't until much later, when I was fourteen, that I began playing goal.

"I was on a team of kids three years older than I was. I remember my mom being very, very nervous that I'd get mauled out there. I was small and skinny, and the gloves were way too big. I remember having a one-on-one with a forward, and I came out of the goal and made the save. I probably would have been scared, if I'd had the time to think about it! Anyway, I found that I liked the position, liked the challenge of it. If I had my way, though, I'd still try to play a little in the field—that was fun, too."

Briana Scurry says that when she was a little girl in Minnesota, she played on an all-boys' team. "The boys were the ones that decided I should be in goal," she says. "I guess they figured I'd be less likely to get hurt if I was back there. As we know now, that isn't really how things work—the risk is probably higher. Anyway, over the next few years I did start playing in the field. It was fun, and I was pretty aggressive. I did rip and run, scored goals and had a good time in the field.

"About four years later, I got on a team with a coach that didn't have a goalie. He asked us all if anybody played goal. I said I'd played some. This was

Briana Scurry has been with the WNT for 15 years.

Natasha Kai is proud of her tattoos.

Kate Markgraf played her first game for the WNT when she was 22.

when I was sixteen. Usually, you know, you would split goalkeeping back then because not that many people wanted it. One would play first half, the other would play the second half. But as you get older, you sort of get nudged out or nudged in. It was more likely for me to be in goal. I was good at it, and I liked it—actually, I loved it. I feel completely at home in there. It's hard to explain, I guess, but it's where I feel the most comfortable. So that's where I stayed."

"I Was Becoming Nervous"

From her first game ever, all the way through high school, Kate Markgraf was a skilled forward. But when she was seventeen, the coach on her club team made the decision to put her on defense. "I remember that it was hard at first," she says. "I missed scoring goals. I was used to thinking of myself as a forward. That was who I was."

Markgraf does not deny that her coach's decision made sense, however. "When I was a kid, I could run and dribble, and no one could catch me," she says. "But you know, I got to a higher level, and everyone is fast. Not only didn't I stand out any more as a forward, I couldn't really compete at those higher levels. I didn't have the skill level to stay as a forward. Mostly, I didn't have that natural calming ability with the ball on my foot that a forward is supposed to have. Forwards need to be calm and composed, not worried about what the defender is going to do. They're supposed to turn off those anxieties and go about doing their job. But I found that more and more, I was becoming nervous about the defender."

Homesick

Kristine Lilly is a dynamo on the field, but says she has always been very shy otherwise. She credits her parents for giving her a nudge to try out for things, even though the thought scared her. "My parents didn't push," she says. "But the only time I remember they were urging me on was to go to regional camp. I was too shy, didn't want to go away from home. The camp was in Michigan—very far from where I lived. I was sixteen. They said, 'Just try it, go see what it's like.' So I went. All the way to Michigan. That was my first time away from home, and I was so homesick. Hey, I was homesick when I went to college, too. That was just the way I was, I guess."

"

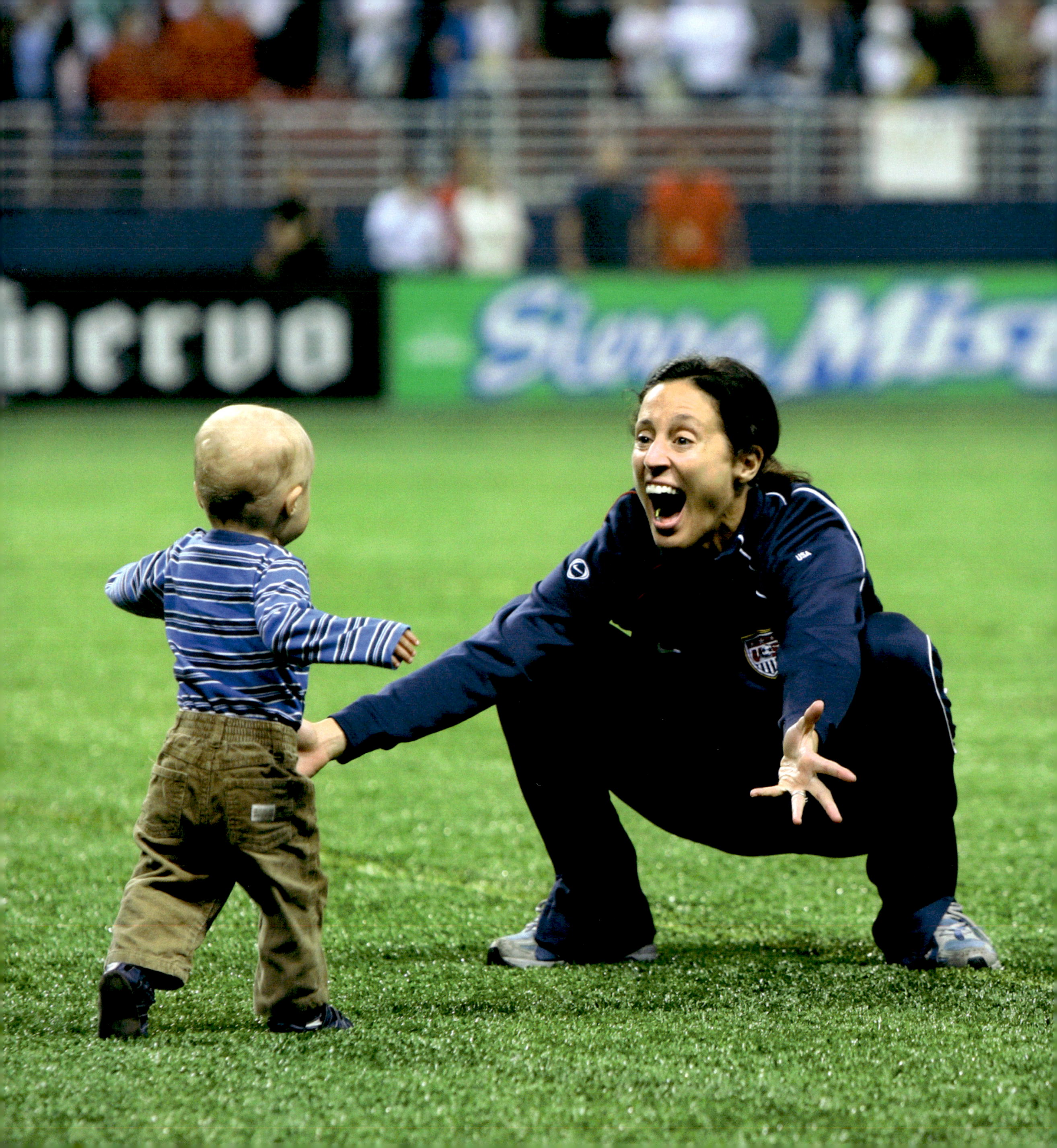

She says that though it was hard to get used to not being a forward, there was an immediate advantage. "I found that I liked watching everything develop. I could see the whole field—who was open, who was making runs, what the defenders were doing. And I could organize things from back there. The calmness I didn't have as a forward, I had as a leader. So now, I'm very comfortable back there, and I'm playing a much different sort of game."

A Tough Balance

As the years went by, coaches began noticing these young women players. For some, making their state and regional ODP teams led to spots on the Youth National Team—where they received more intense training and coaching. That, in turn, led to invitations to the Women's National Team.

Making the team was not automatic, of course. No matter how talented a player had been on a youth team or her college team, finding a spot on the women's team required a big leap in skill and endurance. Ask Kate Markgraf, who says that she learned the hard way how much more fit one has to be to play on that team.

"I was eighteen," she says. "I didn't really know what to expect at the camp. I'd been kind of sick the week before I came in, but I don't know if that was the trouble or not. But the result was, I passed out during the fitness test. We were doing these things called cones—any serious soccer player knows what these are. You do ten repetitions, back and forth to the five, then the ten, and so on. Anyway, I passed out on the eighth repetition. Out cold. I woke up half an hour later, and nobody was there except the trainer.

Markgraf congratulates Hope Solo after a World Cup win against Sweden.

Kate Markgraf greets her son Keegan after a game in St. Louis.

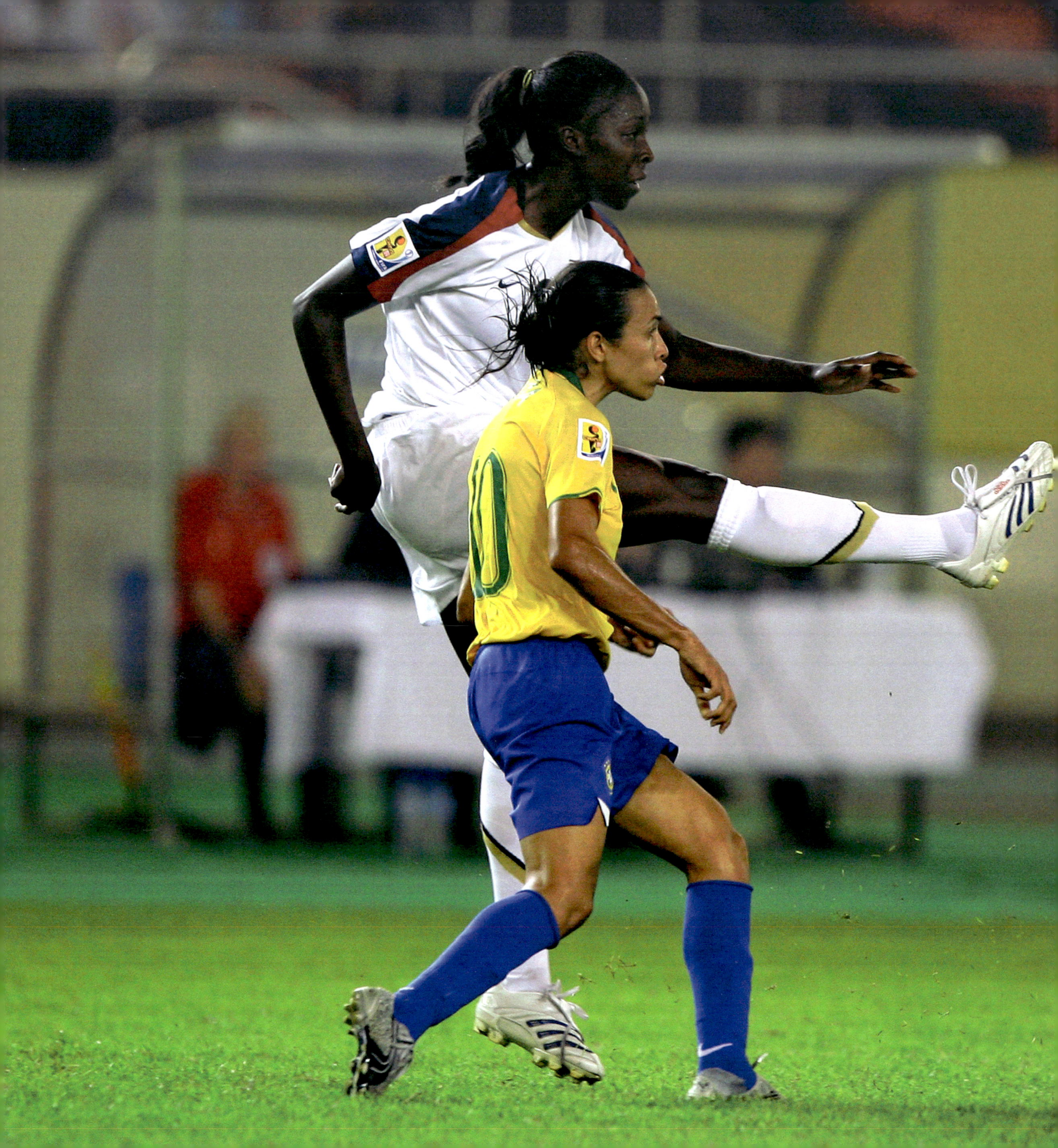

"None of the girls on the team would talk to me. It may sound harsh, but they were completely right. It had been a sign of disrespect to show up unfit. I did not get invited back to tryouts until four years later. And by that time, I was fit. No way was that going to happen to me again. I passed the fitness test with ease."

Another Way

Other players who had not been on national youth teams were noticed on their college teams. Briana Scurry had gotten a soccer scholarship to U Mass, and in her senior year caught the attention of the Women's National Team coach. A week after the college season ended, she was in the National Team camp. "I never imagined that I was good enough to play on that team," she says now. "I was playing so hard in high school, just to get a college scholarship, I didn't even think about it. It just happened, everything worked out right."

For Tina Ellertson, the idea of being on the National Team was far from her mind, too. "I got pregnant my senior year of high school, with my high school sweetheart," she says. "And though I had gotten a four-year college scholarship to Santa Clara, I didn't want to take it. I mean, it's a great, great school, and legendary for its soccer program. But with a new baby on the way I wanted to stay near my family, in Washington state. I ended up going to the University of Washington—not a big-name soccer school."

Tina says that in 2003, she was recruited by Ghana to play on their Olympic team. "I was flattered to be asked," she says, "but by then our daughter MacKenzie was three years old. I was trying to finish up my last year in college. Not a good time to be heading off to Africa."

MacKenzie Ellertson wears her mom's number.

5' 9" Tina Ellertson seems more than a few inches taller than 5' 4" Brazilian star, Marta.

"grandmother's premonition"

Long before Tina Ellertson ever thought about playing for the U.S. National Team, her Nigerian grandmother saw it happening. "She actually saw it, a vision of it, on her deathbed. She told my mother that she could see me playing for the United States, playing with a U.S.A. jersey," says Tina. "She had no reason to think that—there was absolutely no way she could have known that I was going to have an opportunity to do just that. But she was sure. And it happened. The National Team coach saw me play in college, and after I graduated, I made the team. I still get emotional about that, thinking about how my grandmother could have known that."

She stayed in college, and finished her final year. But even though she hadn't been aware of it, the Women's Team coach had heard about her, and had came to one of her college games. He liked what he saw, and soon after graduating she was playing with the the under–21 National Team. And after one or two training sessions, she was moved up to the Women's Team.

Each member of the team can tell her own story of getting on the team, of how she was able to rise to the highest level of women's soccer. The stories of all the team members demonstrate a mixture of determination, dedication—and often—luck. But in the end, it was not important how each got a spot on the team—only that they did it at all.

Stephanie (Lopez) Cox, Tina Ellertson and Lindsay Tarpley visit the Panda Research Station in Chengdu.

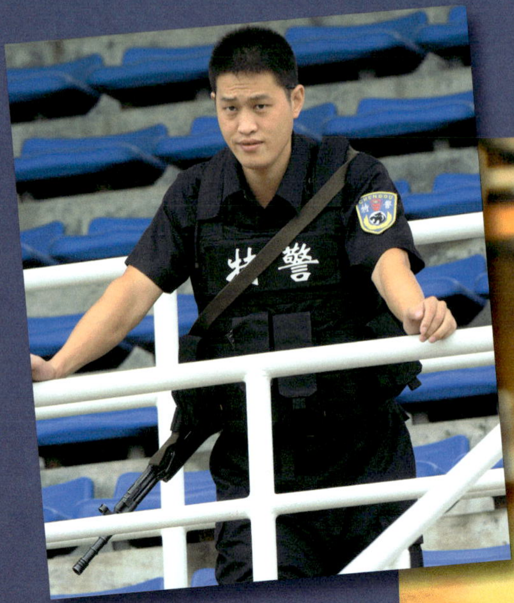
特警
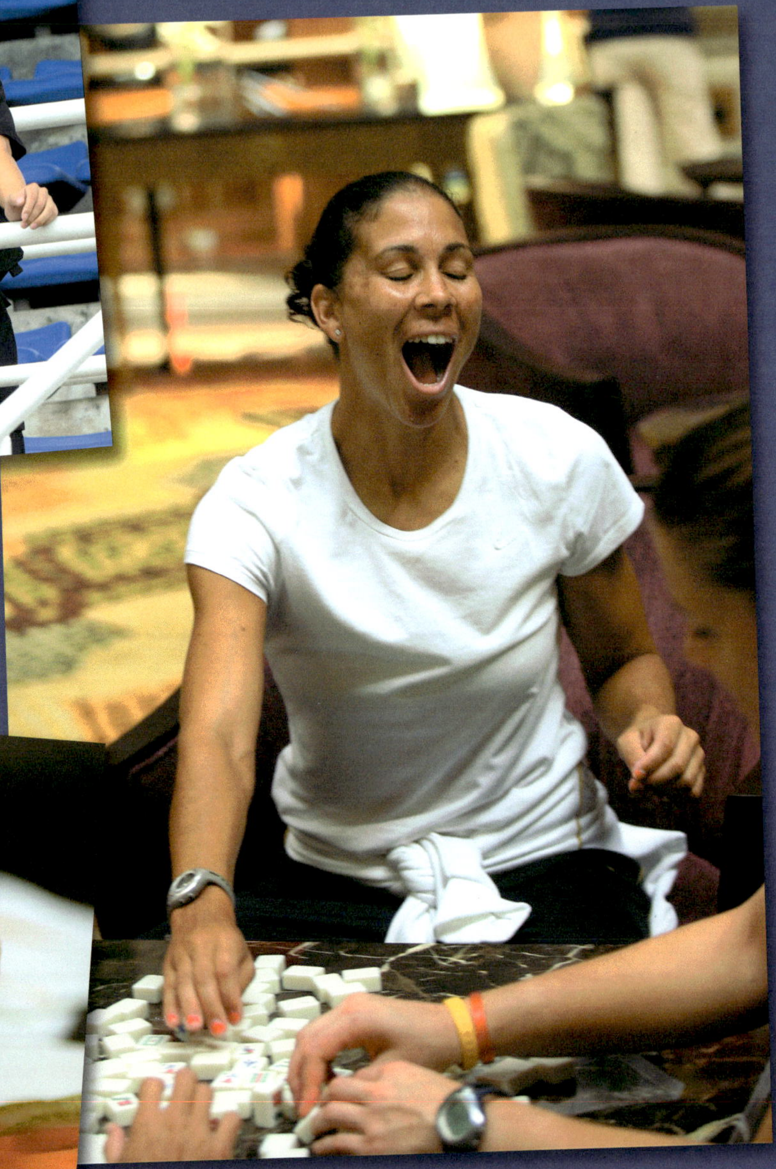
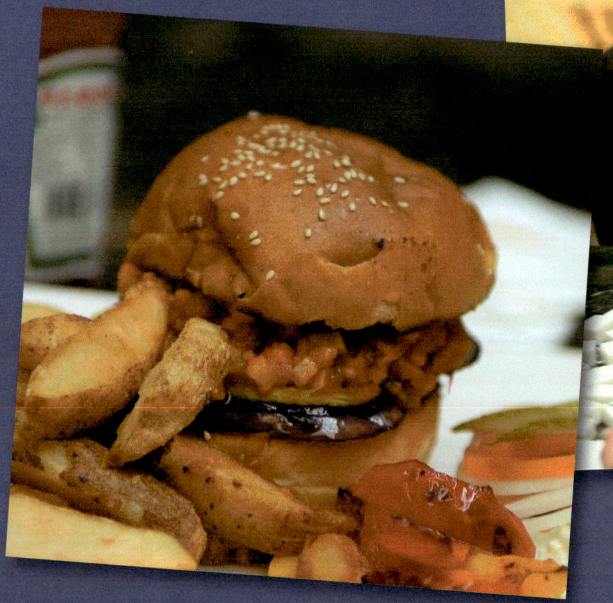

chapter 3

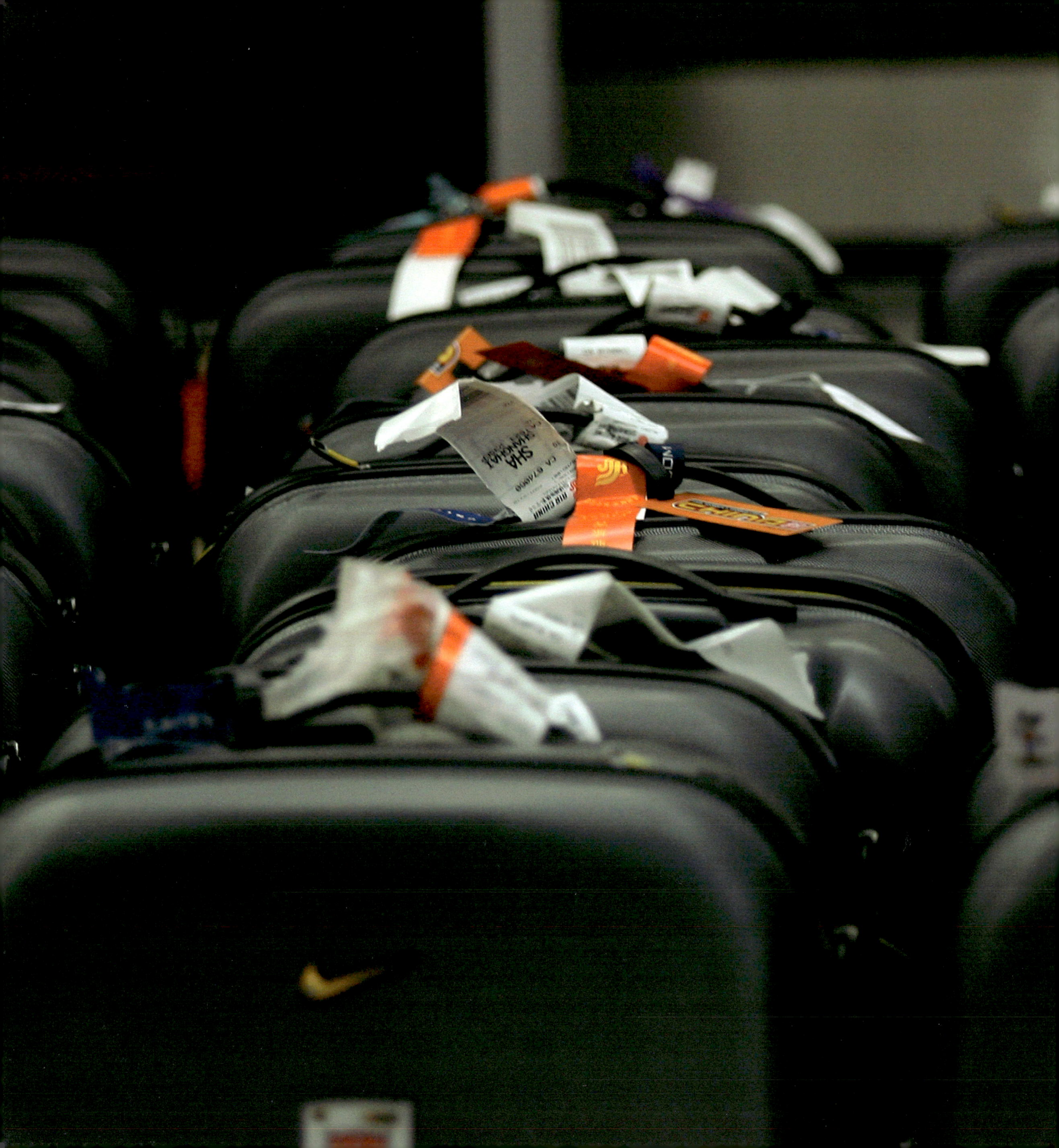
SHA
SHANGHAI

on the road

The U.S. Women's Team that stepped off the plane in China in September 2007 was a mixture of youth and experience, but they were all ready to play. This was the World Cup, and it would be the biggest challenge yet for this fresh new combination of players. As they began their matches, the players also needed to get acclimated to this new environment that was so very different from anything they were used to.

"You're Kind of Amazed Right Off the Bat"

Some of the players had been to China with their Youth National Teams, so they had some idea of what to expect. But many, like Marian Dalmy, were in awe. "It was nothing like I expected," she says. "There were people everywhere, ten times more people than I envisioned. They were outside everywhere, biking, shopping, transporting stuff on their scooters."

The sheer number of people surprised even Heather O'Reilly, who has spent a great deal of time in New York City. "Everyone knows China is highly populated," she says, "but initially, you're kind of amazed right off the bat. I'm used to crowds—more, say, than some of

Angela Hucles and Marci (Jobson) Miller arrive in Shanghai after beating England.

花花旗袍
承接来料加工　Tel:63737814

the girls from the Midwest. But the numbers of bikers, the number of people lining up on the street waiting for buses—I've never seen anything at all like it."

Briana Scurry says that China was unusual not only because of the number of people, but because of the obvious presence of poverty. "The big cities in China are not at all like American big cities," she says. "where there are areas that are nicer, and gradually less nice, and finally really, really poor. In China, you have crumbling buildings that people are living in—and the reason you know they are inhabited is because of the laundry hanging on clotheslines—right next to a five-star hotel. It's the strangest part for me."

"Some of It Was Still Moving"

The food was another aspect of Chinese culture that was a bit difficult to get used to. Many of the players were expecting the food to taste like the Chinese food in the United States—but they soon found out otherwise.

"A lot of us, the newer people, were pretty surprised," admits goalie Nicole Barnhart. But there were a lot of things we couldn't identify, and that was kind of a problem—we just weren't used to it. Like, we'd have banquets, and some of the food was still moving. It was prawns or something, I think."

"You don't want to be judgmental," says Lori Chalupny. "But you find that they eat things on a regular basis that we don't eat. Like you're eating

BEIJING OPERA

chicken, and it looks and smells great, and you look down and there'd be the chicken head in there. Like Nicole said, it's just a question of what you're used to. I'm sure at home, we eat things that Chinese people would find not so appealing."

However, some of the players were willing to try the unusual foods. Angela Hucles says it was just part of the China experience. "I'm not picky," she says. "I love food. The World Cup—that was a long time for us to be away from food we're used to, after all. [In China] they get the fish right out of the water, put it in a paper bag, and cook it. Some people didn't like that, but it's just the way they do it. I'll try anything once."

To make sure the players got enough to eat, the team brought a large trunk filled with more traditional American fare—macaroni and cheese, tuna, crackers, pretzels, and cookies.

Off the Field

There are other aspects of daily life that are important to a team on the road. It's not only a matter of having the tastiest meals or the best hotel, players insist. What is most crucial is that the players feel comfortable and relaxed when they are not on the field. "After all, we spend most of the time when we're on the road not playing," says Natasha Kai. "But all that time in between, you have to find a balance so we can all stay focused for the games coming up. That's really important."

There were a number of things that kept players grounded and balanced. For instance, the presence of family members in China was enjoyable.

Natasha Kai shops in the Old City section of Shanghai.

Heather O'Reilly models a Chinese Opera Mask.

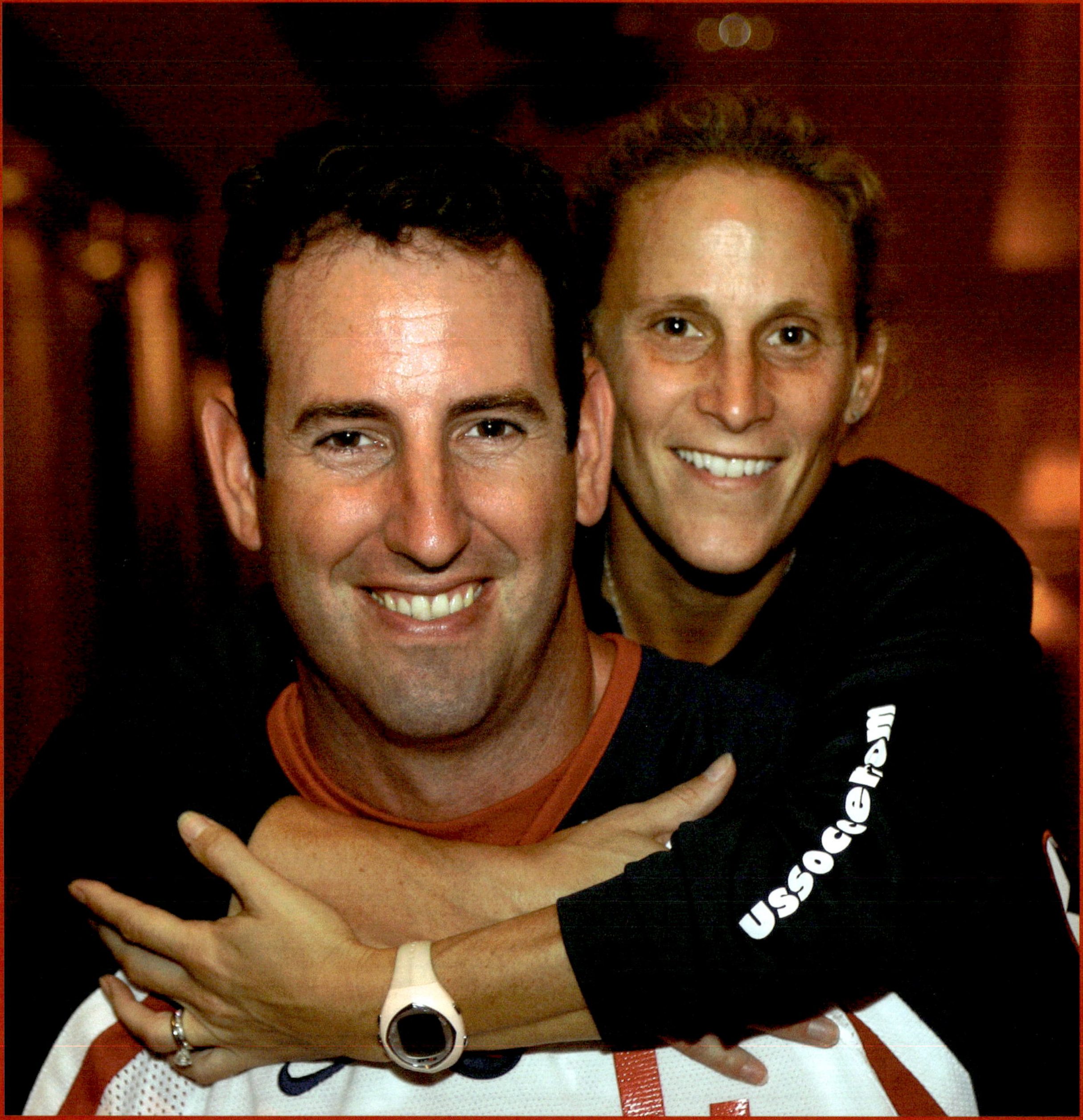
ussoccer.com

Though family did not stay with the players in the hotel, they were able to spend some time having a meal together, shopping, or sightseeing. Kristine Lilly's husband came to China, and she says it meant a great deal to her. "This is the first World Cup since we've been married," she explains. "It was really great to have him there."

Christie Rampone's daughter Rylie came, too. "She turned two when we were in China," says Rampone. "But you know, almost from the time she was born, she was traveling with me. She's absolutely the biggest thing in my life. She's my distraction from all the drama, all the nervousness and anxiety, and that's helped me fall in love with the game of soccer in a completely different way. She's always been easy, happy most of the time. She's a good sleeper, a good traveler, and adjusts well to different time zones—a real bonus!"

Tina Ellertson's six-year-old daughter MacKenzie made the trip, too, and provided a sense of normalcy for her. "It made everything more fun for me, having her there," Ellertson says. "She and Rylie got to be best friends. And my husband and MacKenzie did lots of sightseeing, and took lots of pictures. When they got back home, MacKenzie did a PowerPoint presentation for her first grade class. She was proud of herself. And she hasn't taken off her new backpack with the Chinese letters on it."

Ellertson, reflecting a moment, says that MacKenzie benefited from the experience in a more important way. "Every minute she has spent with me and this team has made an impact," she says. "She's had the opportunity to be around twenty-one strong women. What great role models for her. She's been incredibly lucky, having been able to experience that."

2-year-old Rylie Rampone takes a nap.

Tina Ellertson and daughter MacKenzie.

Kristine Lilly with husband David Heavey.

Twenty Great Aunts

Christie Rampone's daughter Rylie turned two during the World Cup, and the team members (who called themselves the Great Aunts) had a birthday party for her.

"It was so great," says Rampone. "When we sang to her, she had this big smile from ear to ear. She got awesome presents—Marci and Nicole gave her a scroll with the symbol of the year she was born in Chinese. And Tash gave her a Dora the Explorer backpack that she loves."

Time Spent Learning New Things

When not with family, the players found other things to do. Shannon Boxx got hooked on Kristine Lilly's DVDs of *Rescue Me*, a television show about firefighters. Leslie Osborne did what she always does on the road—edits videos and photos on her computer. Many read or watched soccer videos.

Several decided the time could best be spent learning something new. "Four or five of us had a plan that we could use our down time learning Spanish," says Heather O'Reilly. "This was going to be our goal. We started out pretty well—we packed Spanish books and started off exchanging some vocabulary sheets. And I—who have wanted to be a teacher even when I was a little kid—got into making up quizzes for everyone. It kind of faded out though, which was too bad."

"Tash [Natasha Kai] taught us a game called mahjong," says Christie Rampone. "She'd learned it from her family, and we really got addicted. We played at least an hour or two every day we were in China."

Rampone shops for pearls

Top: Rampone fixes Leslie Osborne's hair at the airport.
Above: Kristine Lilly plays mahjong.

Left to right: Cat Whitehill; Christie Rampone and daughter Rylie; Heather O'Reilly

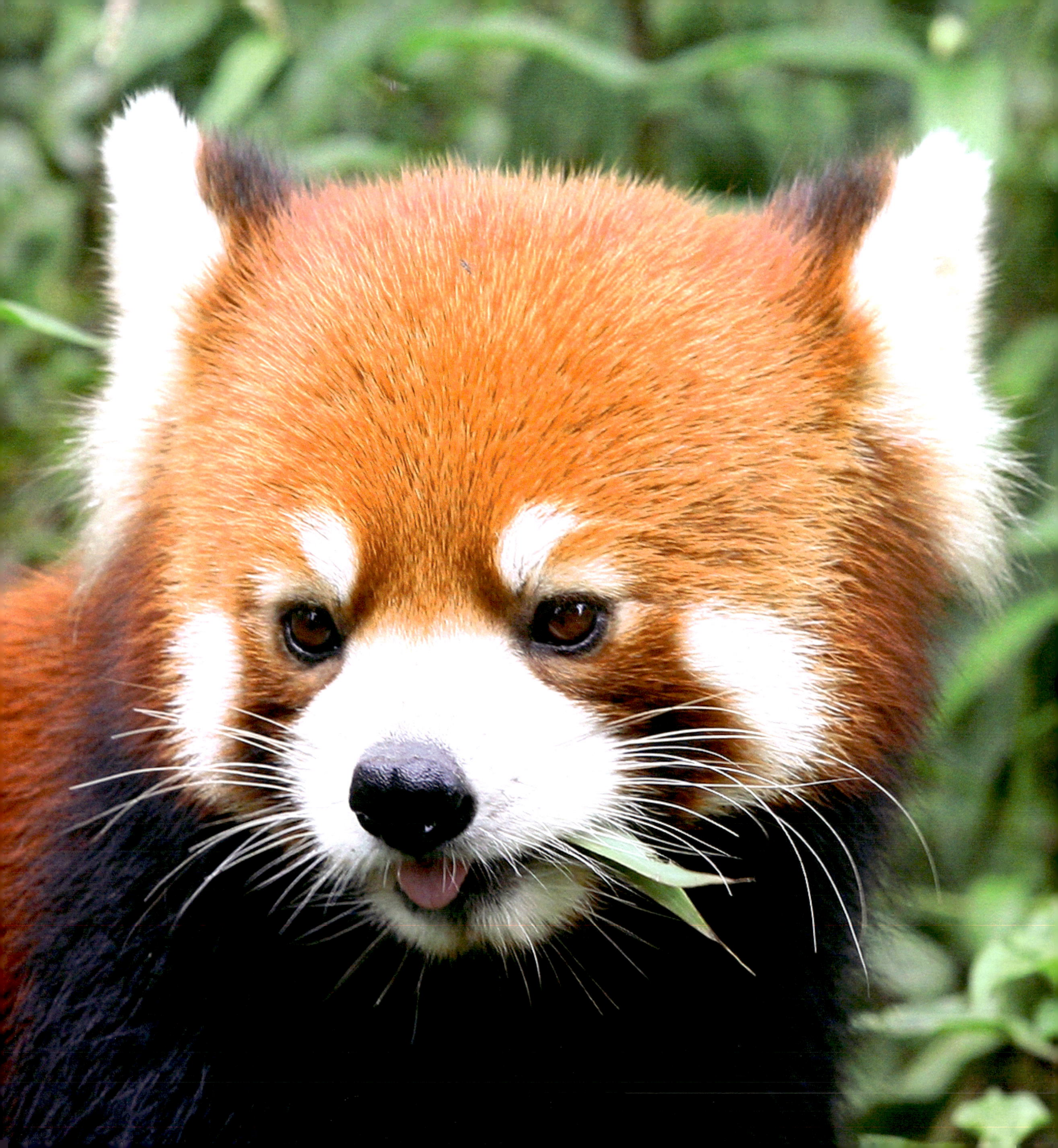

Panda-mania

Ask this team what the highlight of the trip was, and most will mention the pandas. An endangered animal, pandas roam freely in a special research preserve not far from the soccer venue in Chengdu. Shuttles move through the preserve, allowing visitors to see the pandas in a natural, protected habitat.

Nicole Barnhart says it was hands-down the best part of the trip. "They had a special kindergarten for the young pandas, where they can do lots of tumbling and climbing. They're really amazing. We got to sit next to one of the older pandas. We could even touch him, but we had to wear plastic gloves so we didn't transmit any diseases or germs. I'll always remember that."

Marian Dalmy was struck by how tiny the newborns were. "You can see them behind glass," she says. "That was unforgettable. Their fur is all white; I guess it takes a while for the black to come in."

Leslie Osborne, who never imagined any animal being as lovable as golden retrievers, says that after seeing the pandas, she purchased a toy stuffed panda. "They are my second favorite animal now," she insists. "The panda I bought is half my size, and traveled everywhere with me in China, everywhere we went. I'll keep it forever. My team thought it was hilarious, but I didn't care."

Giant panda checks out the visitors.

A red panda eats bamboo at the Panda Research Station in Chengdu.

Leslie Osborne holds her all-time friend.

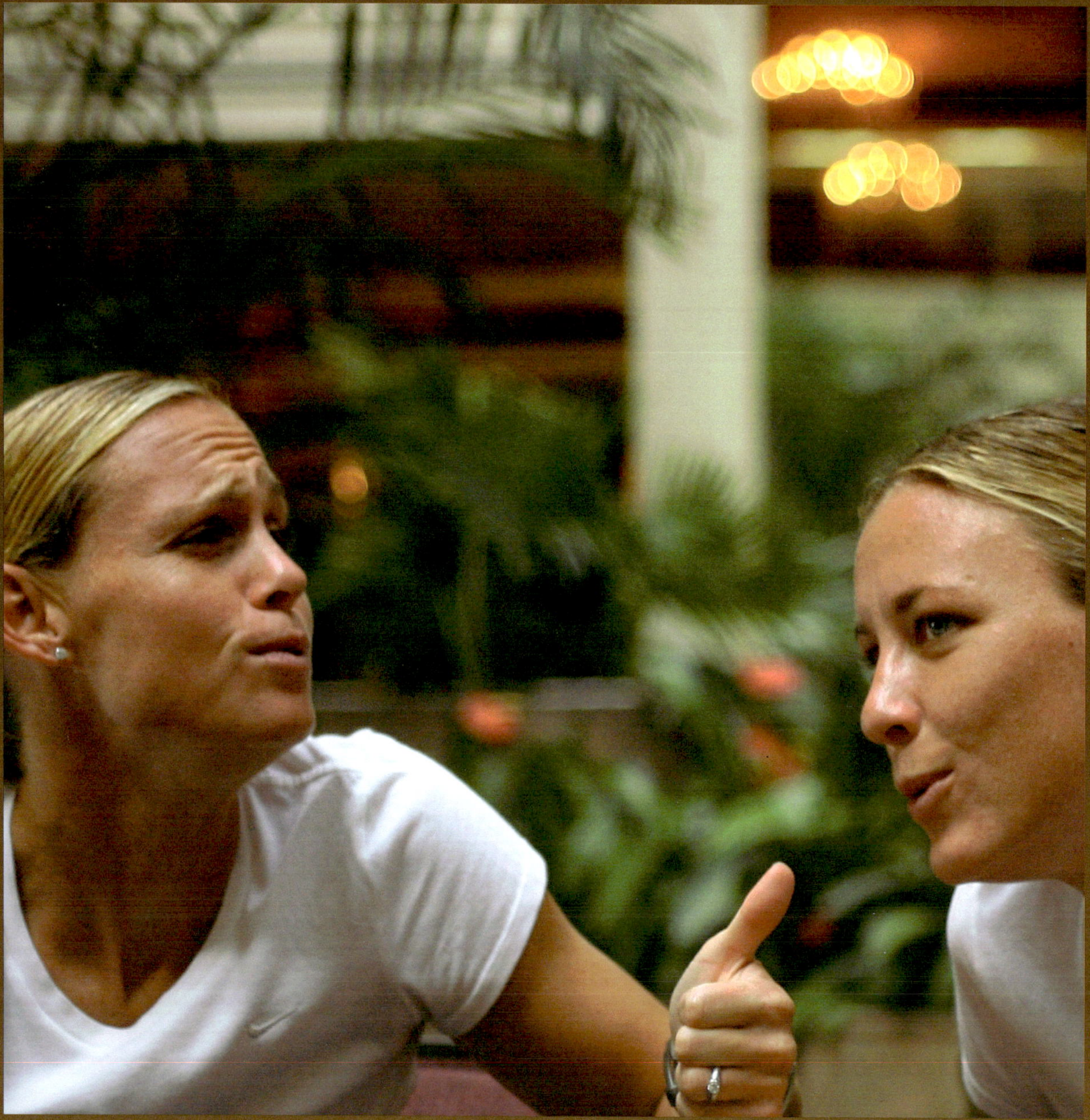

The Quiet Highlight

But there was one aspect of the trip that was less spectacular, but just as meaningful to many of the players. "It wasn't anything big," says Lindsay Tarpley. "But the best part for me was just those quiet times, hanging out with teammates at the hotel. Just talking."

"Some people spend years and years playing on a team, and never really get to know their teammates," adds Angela Hucles. "But this team is the best—a bunch of us having those late evening conversations about whatever comes to mind. I'd agree that that was one of the best things about this trip."

Abby Wambach couldn't agree more. "I grew up around some of these women," she says, "And as much as I have enjoyed the soccer, I have to say that I have learned as much from these talks, just sitting in the hotel room together. I mean, we're not plotting out game strategies. It's just about life—mortgage payments, buying a house, what it's like to have a baby. It makes me feel more than ever that we are a family."

Kristine Lilly paints her nails red and blue, a team ritual.

Christie Rampone and Abby Wambach sing in a Tianjin hotel lobby.

Nail Polish

"My superstition is that when I paint my nails, I don't take off that polish color as long as we win," says Kate Markgraf. "And if we keep winning, it just doesn't come off, regardless if there's just a speck of it left. The polish is always red and blue—alternate fingernails."

Shanghai Hongkou Football Stadium where games against Nigeria and Norway were played.

Game Time

That relaxing flow of conversation was not in evidence on game days. Each of the players needed to calm jittery nerves in the hours before the opening whistle—and most of the time, that was a solitary effort. It was time to retreat into themselves, to find ways to think about the game without obsessing over it, to find just that special mixture of nerves and excitement.

"A lot of us escape into our iPods," says Cat Whitehill. "We have certain music on there that can get us pumped up, or calm us down—depending on what we need. And it changes all the time. For the China trip, I had songs by Kanye West, I had Linkin Park on there. I was really into the song 'All That I'm Living For' by Evanescence. Everybody has their own, and when we ride over to the field, it seems like most of us are plugged in, just finding that zone, I guess you'd call it."

Unlike many of her teammates, Briana Scurry found it more helpful not to fight the nervousness before a game. "I'm someone who doesn't want to relieve that stress," she says. "My feeling is that it's a part of passion—it's a key part of the game for me. It's not comfortable—don't get me wrong. But I look at that nervousness as my mind and body letting me know that I'm ready to play. The trick is to channel those feelings, I guess. The one good thing, though, is that you calm down automatically as the game starts—at least I do."

Though most of the players tend to withdraw somewhat before games, not all of the pre-game routine in China was solitary—thanks to the energetic spirit of Natasha Kai. "Tash kind of came up with a special dance routine," says Christie Rampone. She worked it out for six of us, and choreographed the whole

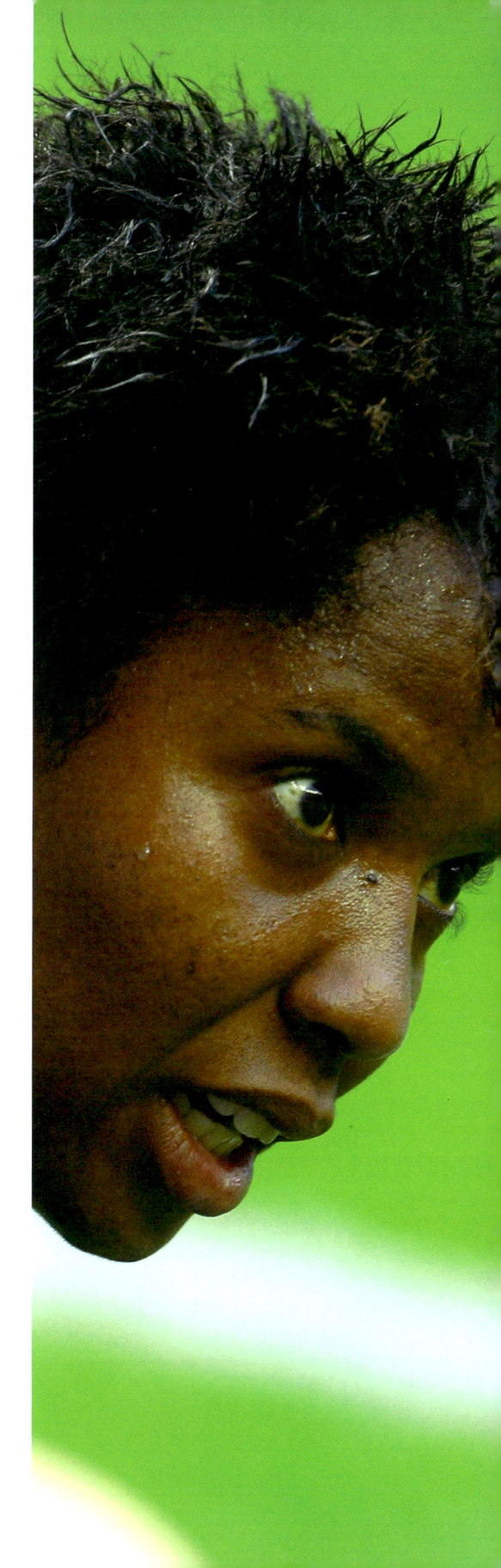

Briana Scurry

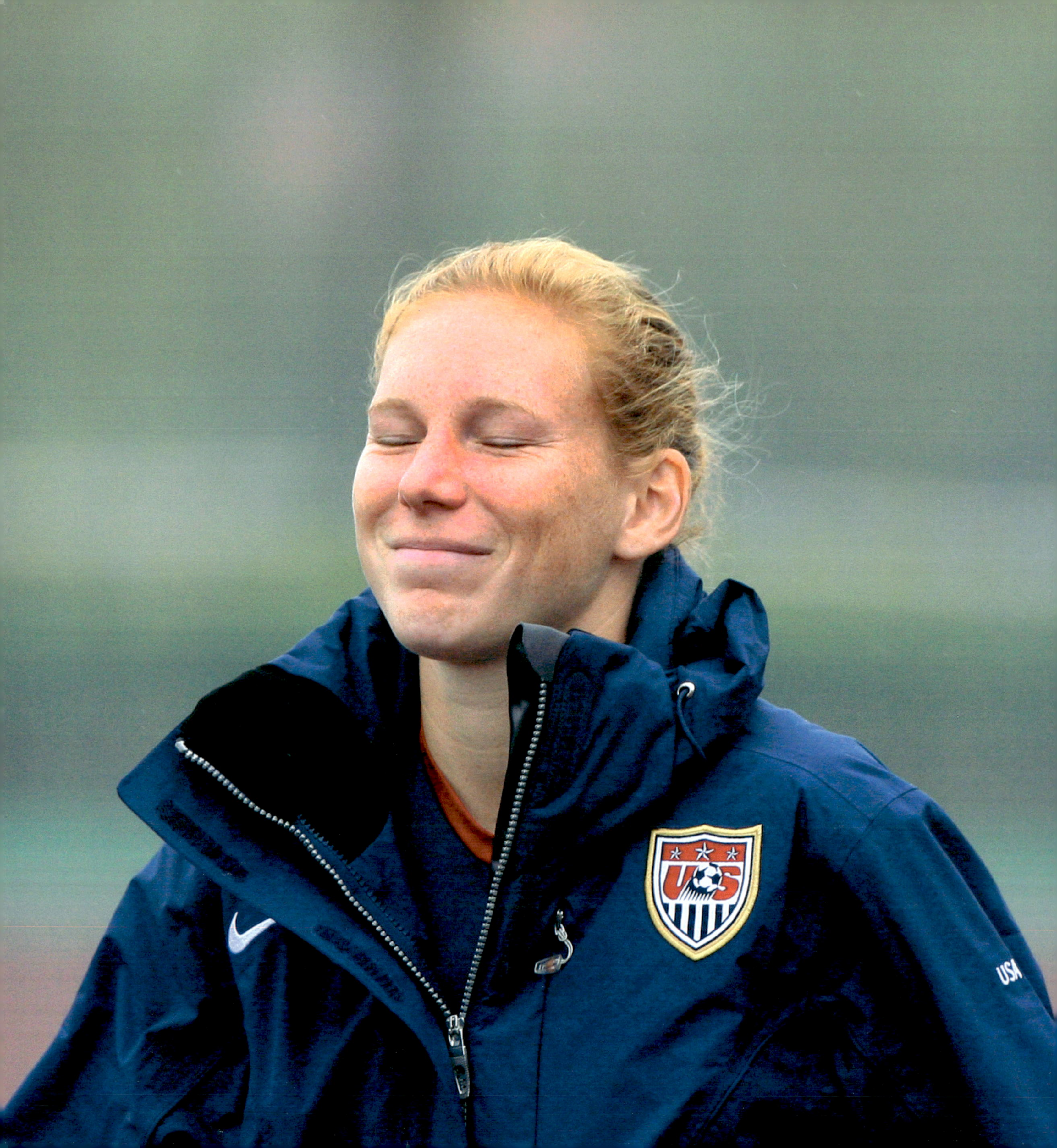
US
USA

thing. We wanted to do it in the locker room before the first game, just to boost everybody up a little. I mean, anything you can do to make the day go by a little faster before the game helps. Anyway, this was fun—after hours of doing nothing but thinking about the game, it was great to get into something funny, to get our mind off stuff for a while, you know? Everybody really liked it—it was fun to laugh."

The Bad Day

There was one well-publicized time when the team's balance went out of whack. It became a problem that threatened to disrupt the chemistry and momentum that the players had worked so hard to achieve. When Coach Greg Ryan decided to start Briana Scurry in goal against Brazil for the semifinal game, he did so because he felt she had more experience than Hope Solo against Brazil. After the game, which the U.S. lost 4-0, Solo publicly criticized the coach's decision.

Her comments violated an unspoken rule in soccer, which is to never, ever publicly criticize one's coach or disparage a teammate. People all over the world wondered what would happen to the U.S. team, which had seemed so together, so focused. Though they had lost in the semifinal, there was still a game to be played for third place. Could they win? And did anyone on the team still care?

Lori Chalupny enjoys warmups.

Christine Lilly congratulates Abby Wambach after a goal against Sweden.

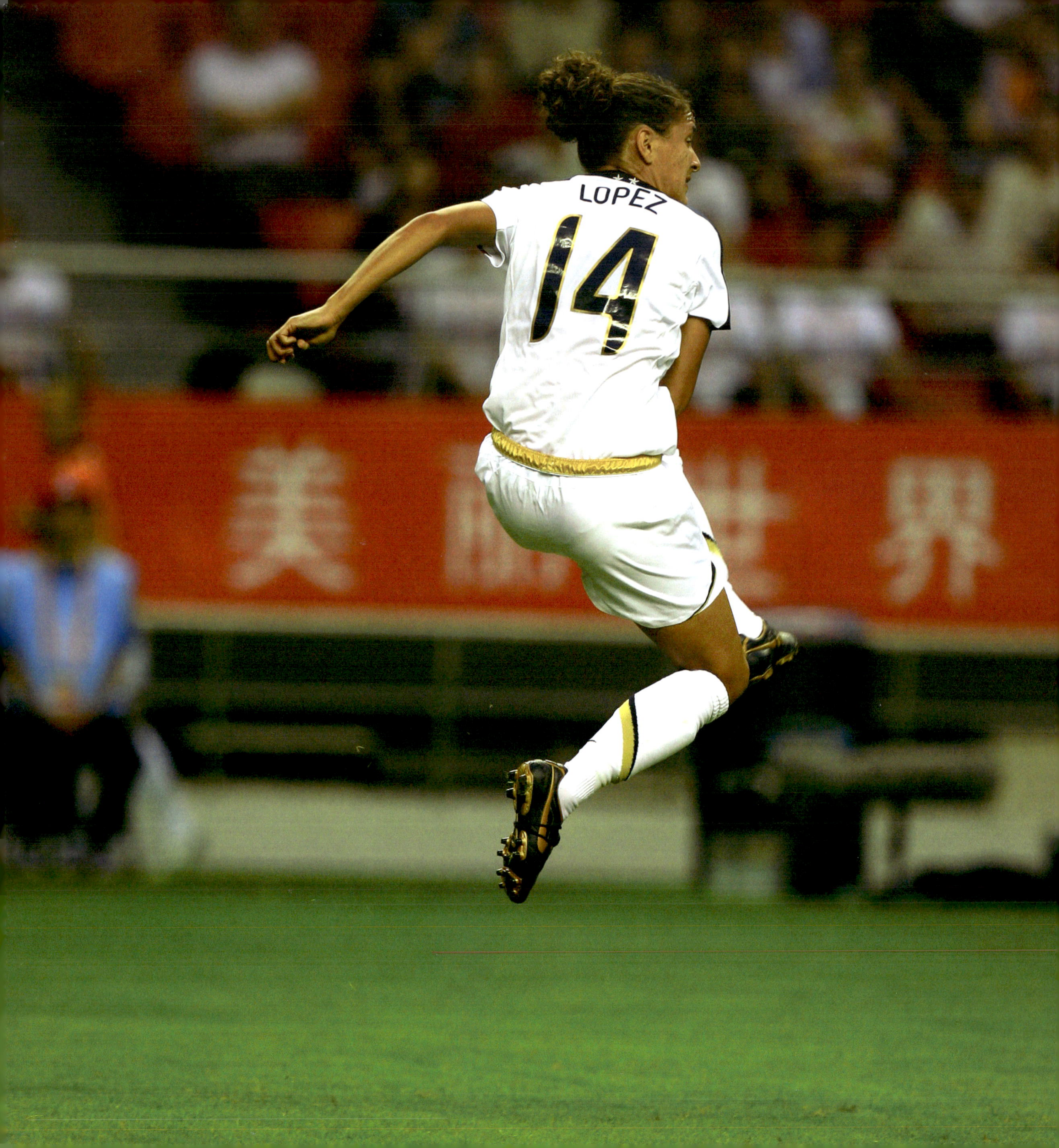
LOPEZ
14

"There Were People Setting Their Clocks for 4:00 a.m."

The answer was evident in the next game, as fans watched the U.S. team play superb soccer, beating Norway for third place. But for the team, says Lori Chalupny, the answer came much earlier. "We gave ourselves twenty-four hours after that Brazil game to feel sorry for ourselves, to feel mad at what had happened," she recalls. "We all had meetings and said how we felt. It was a time we needed to start healing, but we didn't have the luxury of taking too long to do it. Plus, we knew there were a lot of fans back home that wanted to see us win that third place game. Back in the United States, there were people setting their clocks for 4:00 a.m. [because of the time difference] so they could see it live. They're not giving up on us, and they deserved our best."

Even people who normally don't speak out were asked to talk. "That would be me," says Christie Rampone. "I really don't usually do much talking in times of conflict—I'm not comfortable doing that. But here, I had to give an opinion because I was asked to. So I stepped out of my comfort zone. Actually, I think a lot of people listened because I don't usually talk much. But like I said, I had to this time, for my teammates.

Though they prefer that the opinions and statements made during the meetings

Abby Wambach scoring sequence in win over Norway.

Stephanie (Lopez) Cox goes up to volley the ball in 2007 World Cup Norway game.

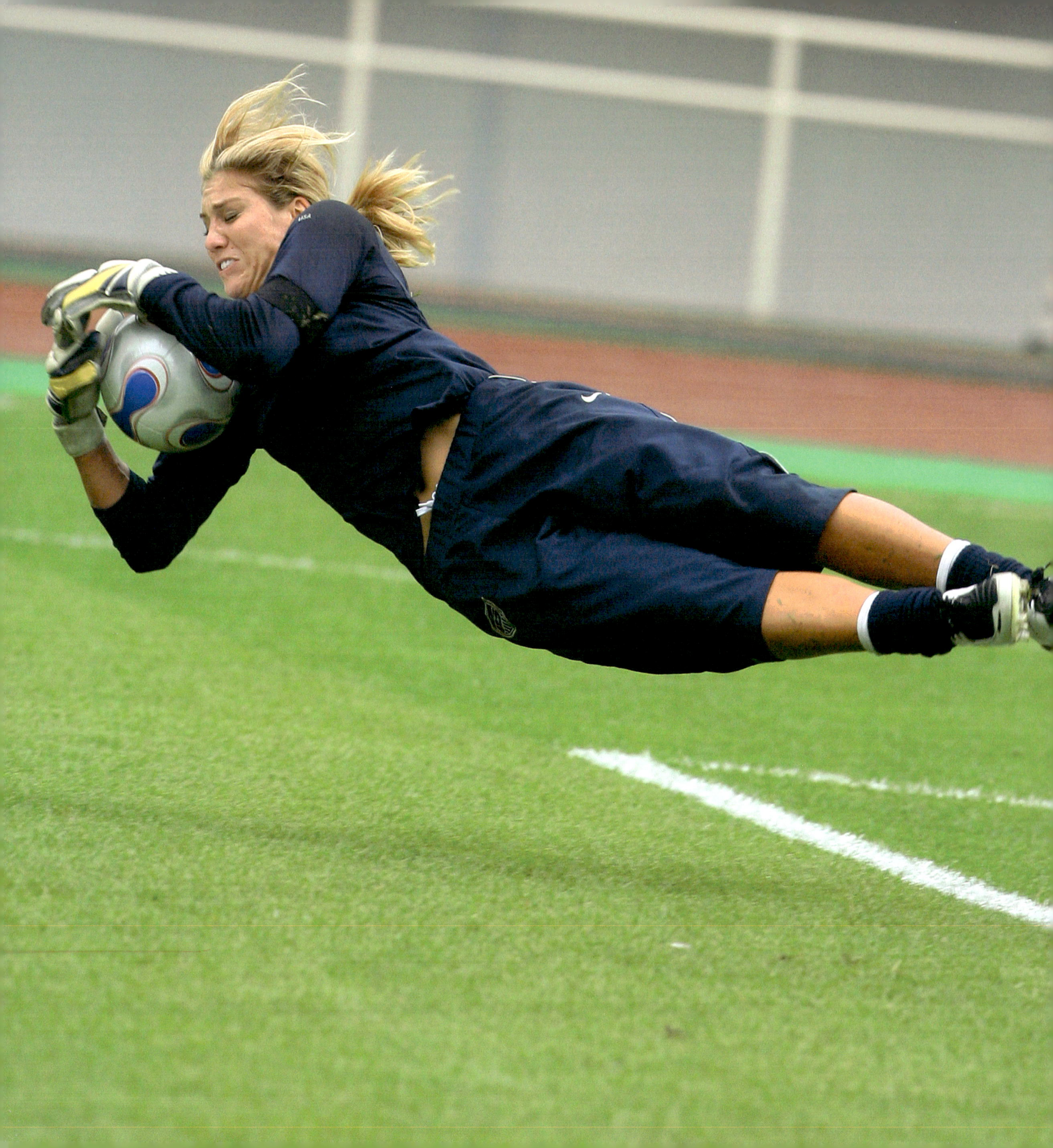

remain private, team members say the main idea was that the team was more important than any one person. "It's the soccer tradition on this team," says Stephanie Lopez. "It's always been there, but it's at times like these, when it's tested, that it helps to think about how valuable it is. I mean, even back when Mia Hamm was on this team—the star player—she always pointed back at her teammates for her successes. It's not about ego, not about personal stats. On this team, everybody is good, everybody is used to being a star. But nobody—nobody—is above the team."

Tina Ellertson credits Kristine Lilly as being the catalyst who brought the team together in those hours before the Norway game. "She just exudes strength and leadership," says Ellertson. "She cares so much about the team's legacy—I mean, she's been on the team for twenty years, so she's pretty much written it. She called us together before the last game. She wanted us to end this tournament with our heads up, proud. Maybe a lot of teams could shrug off a third-place game, like once they lost in the semifinal, they didn't care. But we would play well. Right there, I thought, I'm seeing leadership at its best."

"We Just Looked in Each Other's Eyes"

Once the game was over—the result a convincing 4-1 win for the U.S. team—there would still be important work to do in healing the delicate bonds between members of the team. But no one doubted that the healing would happen. "It was way too quiet, leaving China," says

Solo comes down gracefully after a goal kick.

A Devastating Loss

Just weeks before the team left for China, Hope Solo got a terrible phone call. "It was the coroner's office, telling me my dad had died," she says. "It was so unexpected, and I was so sad. He was really proud of my soccer, but hadn't seen me play yet on the National Team. That night, he was supposed to come watch me play a match in New York. Afterwards we were going to go around to the Bronx, to see his old neighborhood."

She says that with the World Cup trip coming up, she never really had time to grieve for her father. "Not until I came home," she says. "That's when I had time to deal with it. It has made a difference for me. Priorities were different. No soccer game could ever have the same life-and-death importance. It's a perspective I'd never had before. And another thing—since that night, I still haven't been able to relax when the phone rings."

Rampone. "I mean, we'd settled some of it, but the emotions were raw, you know? Like when you have a fight with a friend, or whatever. You settle the argument, but it takes awhile for those emotions to feel settled. I had no doubt that things would be okay, though."

Hope Solo later apologized for her comments, and insisted that she never meant to criticize fellow goalie Briana Scurry—only the coach's decision. "Briana is a very, very strong and forgiving person," says Solo. "When we saw each other again [after the World Cup], when I walked into the room, she came up to me first. She gave me a big hug, we just looked in each other's eyes and kind of nodded. Then I knew it was okay."

In a way, some team members later noted, the whole experience, while unpleasant, had value. "We showed the world who we are," says Heather O'Reilly. "We lost a game. A couple tough games and one big loss, but hey, we're still the United States, and we're not going anywhere. That was a very strong message, that we came back and played with class. I'm proud of our team."

"Things are better with our team after China," says Natasha Kai. "I mean, we talk about how this team is like family sometimes, and it is. But sometimes we mean it only in a good way, like that means we always get along. But real families have their ups and downs. Things go out of whack, but at the end of the day, you're still a family. These girls are my sisters. Hope is still my girl. People make mistakes—who doesn't? But we aren't going to break that bond."

Heather O'Reilly in travel mode.

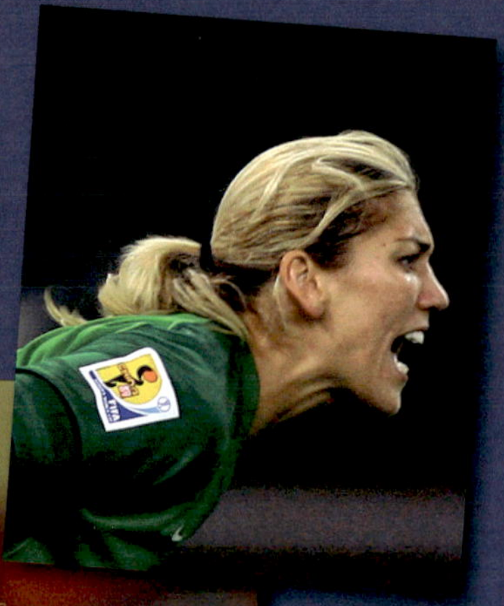
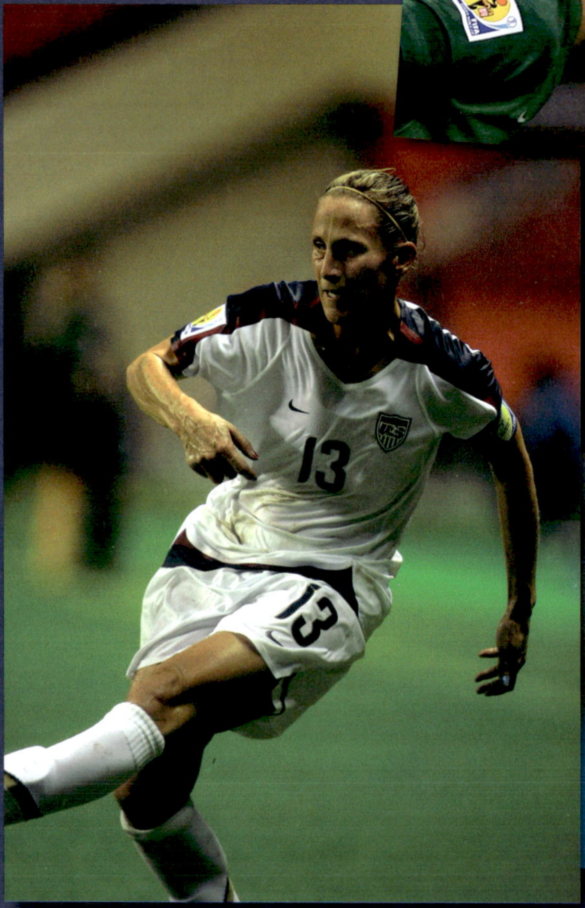
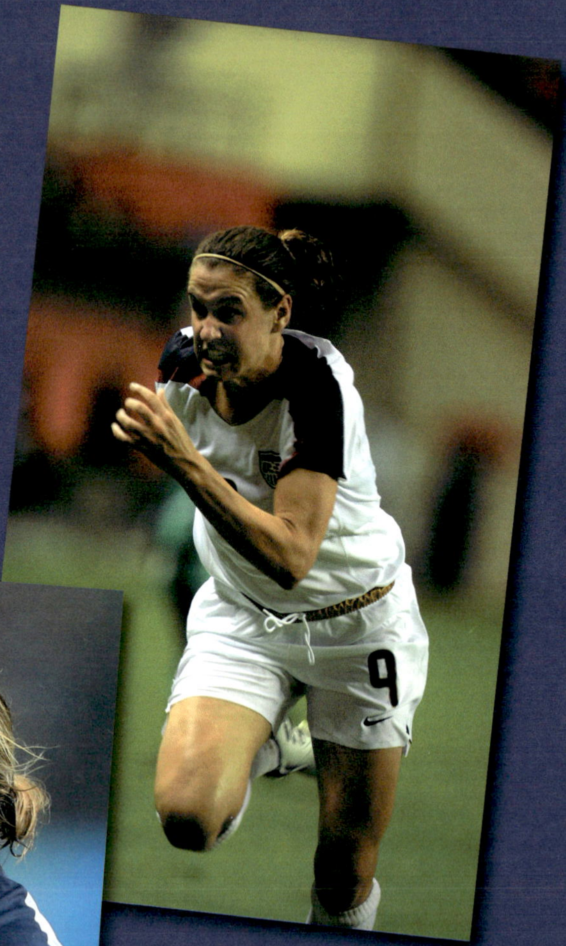
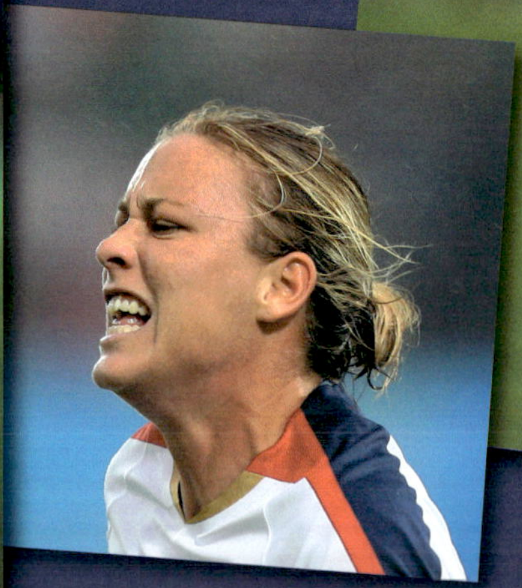

chapter 4

Aly Wagner had ACL surgery when she was 17.

challenges

The challenge the players overcame at the World Cup was difficult, partly because it was so public. But the members of this team have had to deal with challenges before—some of them far worse. And because these difficulties were usually private ones and didn't receive press coverage, they went unnoticed by others.

It is almost impossible to play soccer—or any sport—without experiencing setbacks and problems. And, say team members, it is important for players to understand that. The challenges can range from slumps to injuries, from sitting on the bench to losing interest in the game. But these are all part of the game, they say. Not the fun part, but part of the game nonetheless.

Bad Game

It happens to every player, even those at the highest levels of the sport—matches when even the most elementary aspects of the game are bungled and blown. The result? Poor passing, shots that arc high over the goal, and a growing lack of confidence. The puzzle of having bad game—more a psychological challenge than a physical one, but that doesn't make it any easier to solve.

"The thing that happens is that the harder you try to fix it, the worse it seems to get, and you start losing confidence," says Abby Wambach. "What I try to do when that happens is to scale back a little. See, I know that I can

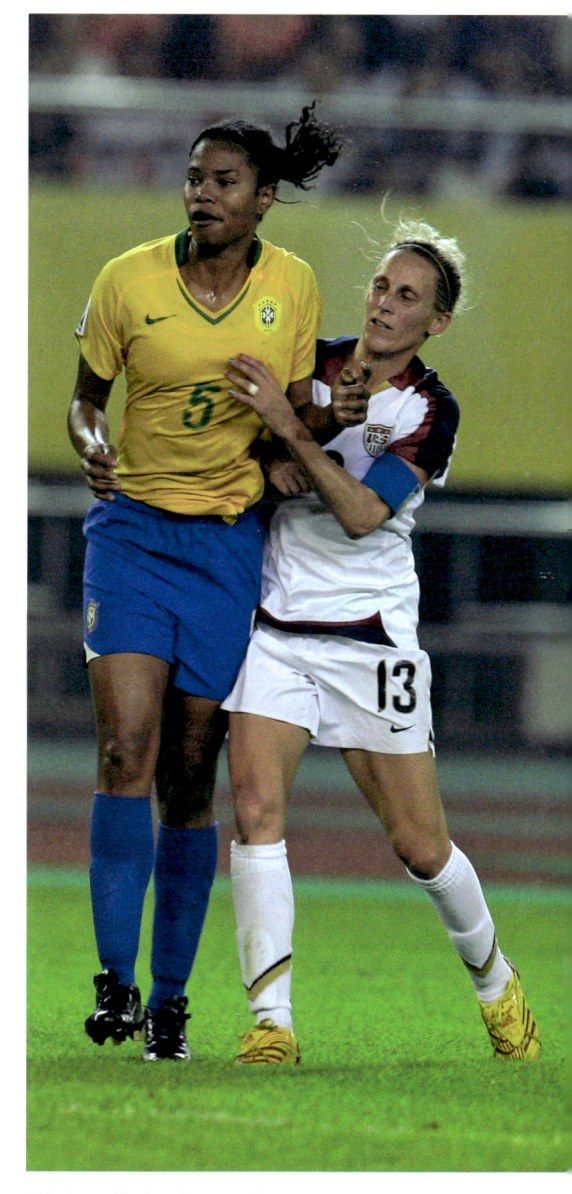

Kristine Lilly battles Brazil's Renata Costa for position.

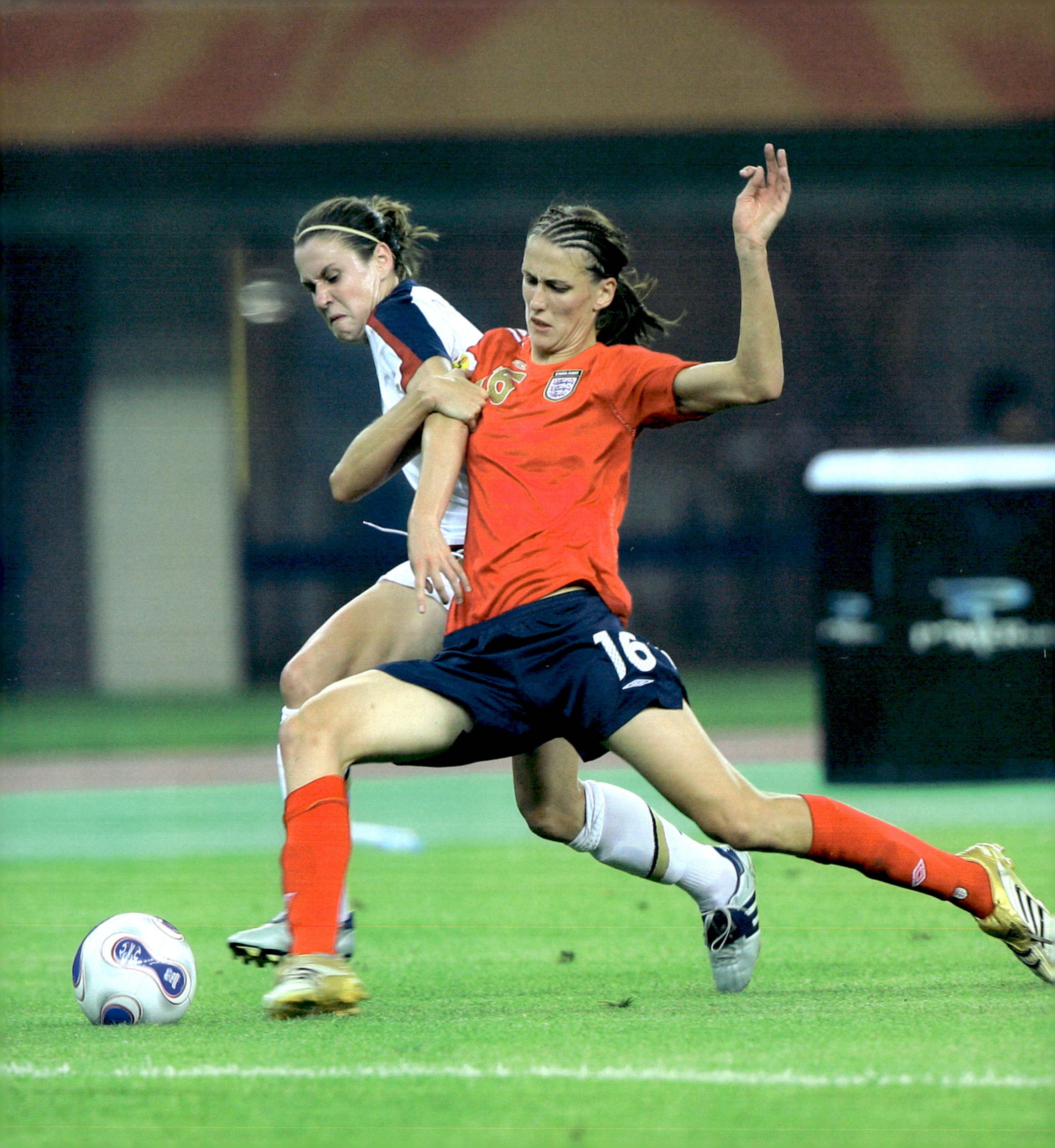
16

always fall back on some part of my game—making a run, making a good pass, whatever—until I get my confidence back. That way I can work my way back to playing the way I like to play."

"You just learn to shrug it off," says Lori Chalupny. "Nobody can play a game without making mistakes. The higher levels, people just learn to deal with it, I think. After a game, I can remember just about every bad play I made, but during the game, I just go on. I guess I've learned that if I'm not making mistakes, I must not be putting myself out there, risking anything."

Heather O'Reilly agrees about the risks, but feels that it may have something to do with the position she plays. "Sometimes my tendency is to get more cautious. But as a forward, I don't think that works for me. I have been talking to a coach back home, who recommended that I write COURAGE on my wrist, to remind me when I'm on the field and not playing well, or things just aren't going well and I'm not taking risks. I think that's what makes a player special, to take risks. It's important to leave your comfort zone and try something different. Challenge yourself, and that's how you grow as a player."

For her, as a forward, that means attacking. "COURAGE for me means taking a defender on, one on one. Or maybe taking a shot I might normally pass off. I try to be a game changer, rather than wait for someone next to me to do it. It's tough to do—when you're playing badly, playing courageously isn't easy. But I think it's a good thing to try."

Lori Chalupny looks for a pass.

Heather O'Reilly battles for position against England.

Abby Wambach beats a Swedish defender to start a run.

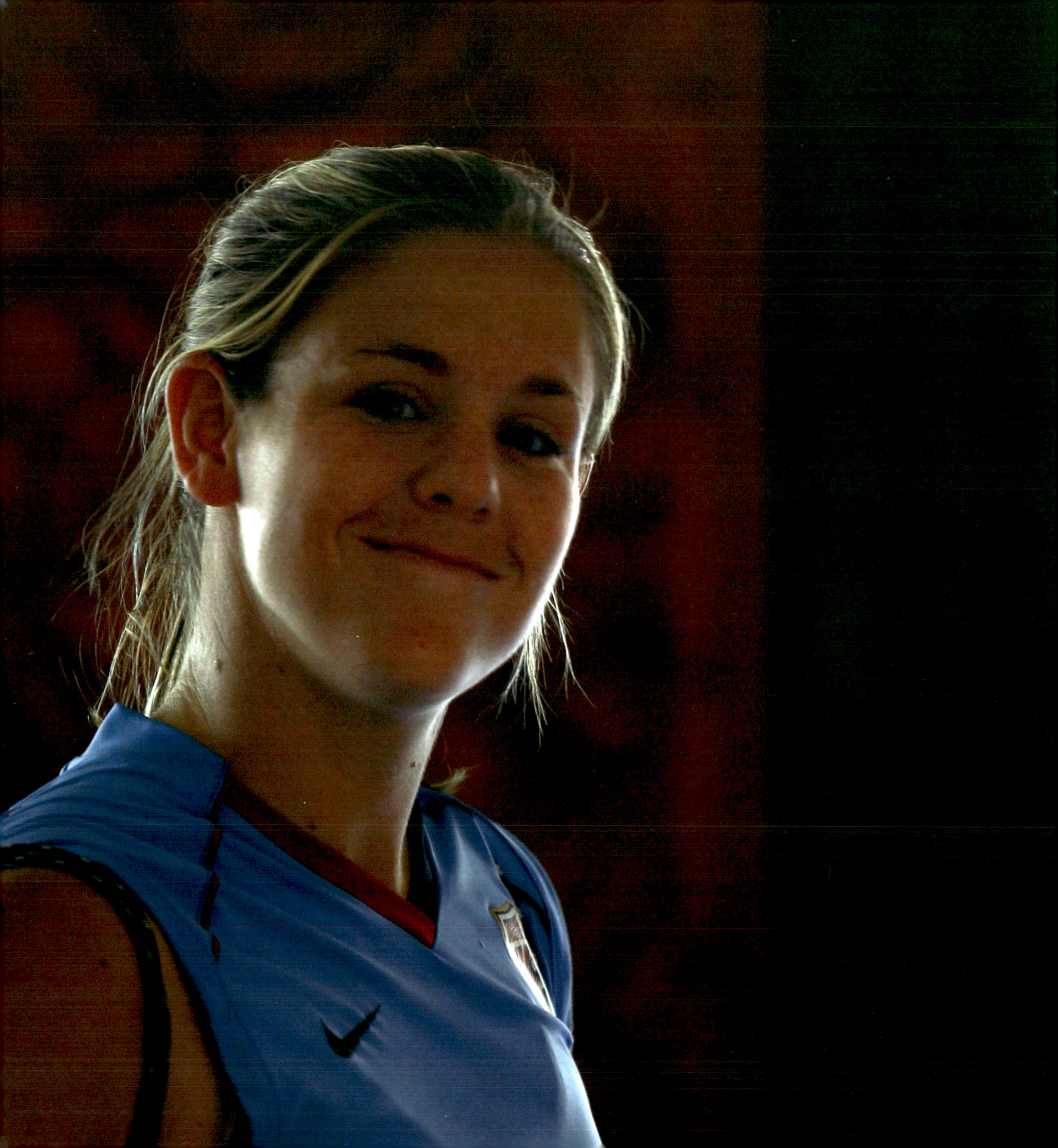

"We've All Felt It"

While there are various ways to deal with the problem, players say that teammates are usually part of the solution. "We've all felt it when we're playing badly," says Kristine Lilly. "Those players around you can carry you for a little, get you back into the routine. When it's someone near me that's struggling, I might try to get them to laugh a little, not to take it too seriously. It does feel serious though, and at this level, when you're playing bad, you get pulled, and that can be hard on your confidence."

Cat Whitehill says that players have different needs when they are struggling. "For me, it helps in the middle of a game to remember that I've got someone right next to me that I know is going to cover for me. People are supportive on this team—they don't guilt you, which is great. You hear about that happening on other teams, and that's bad. I mean, the last thing you need when you are having trouble is to have teammates making you feel worse.

"On this team, we all know it might be someone else one day, and the next day it could be you. So we are all together. We talked about that in a meeting before the World Cup, how to communicate with one another about that kind of thing. Some people want to hear supportive stuff like 'It's okay, I'm right behind you.' Others want more direct talk, like 'Hey, pick it up—you've got to do better.' Not me. I need support from my team. But it's good to know what people need."

Whitehill shows great form in World Cup game vs. Nigeria

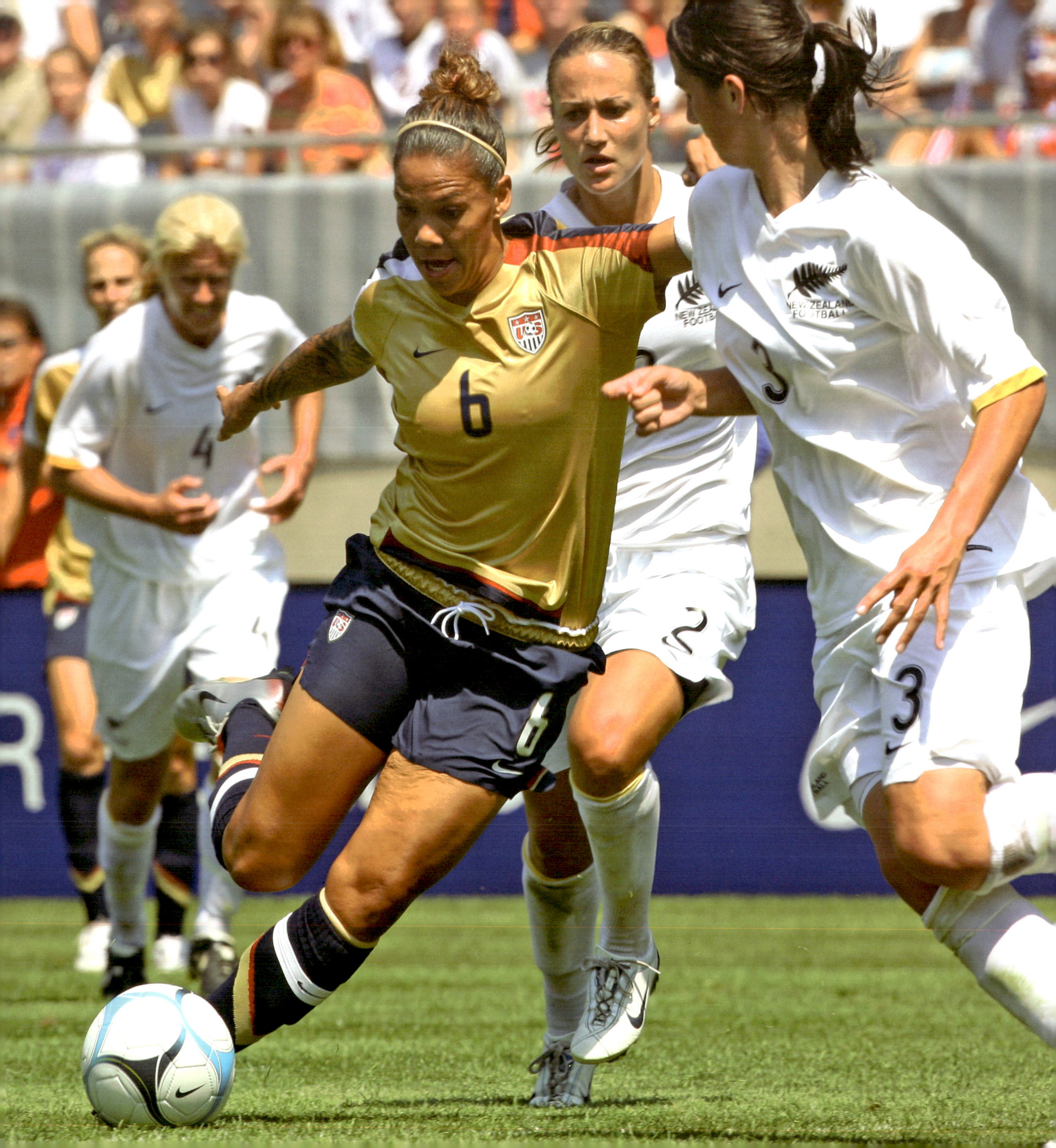
NEW ZEALAND FOOTBALL

"I Can't Do This Right Now"

There is another psychological challenge that is far more serious than a bad game—or even a string of bad games. It occurs when a player simply—inexplicably—loses interest in playing soccer. Evan Meyers is a sports psychologist, and has seen it more times than he can count. "It's like a switch turns off," he says. "It seems to happen without warning. The player wakes up one day and just says, 'I can't do this anymore.' And instead of heading off to college to play the sport he or she has been recruited for, or leaving for training camp after being thrilled to be invited, the player wants to walk—or run—the other way."

That happened to Natasha Kai, right out of high school. "I was really excited when I got offered a full scholarship to the University of Hawaii. It would have been hard for my family to come up with tuition money, so this was great. Everybody made a big deal over my scholarship—no one else in my class had gotten such a great deal."

But what happened? She says she isn't sure. "I just didn't want to go to college. I felt pressure, I guess. Not from my parents, but everyone else. I was overloaded on soccer. It was all I'd thought about in high school, and I think it just came crashing down on me one day that I needed a break. I went to my mom and said, 'Mom, I can't do this right now. If I go, I'll just come right back home.'"

Kai says her mother was understanding. "I know that timing couldn't have been worse. But I talked to the college coach, the one who had recruited me, and it turned out okay. He said he'd hold my scholarship until the next year.

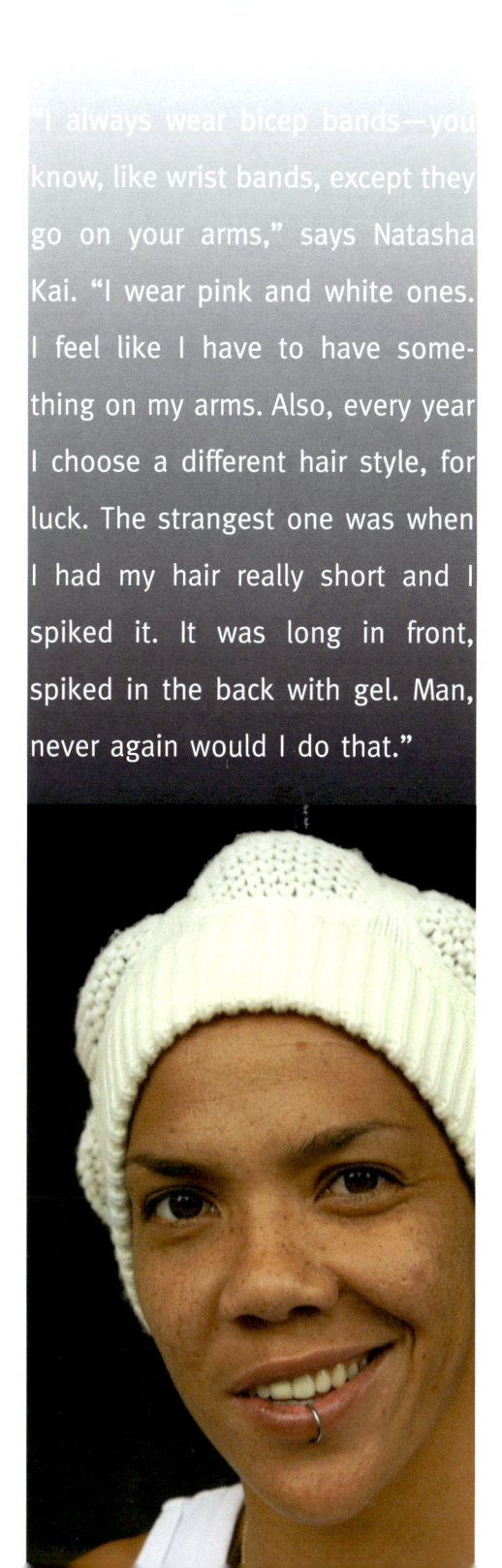

Natasha Kai makes a power move against New Zealand in Chicago.

"I always wear bicep bands—you know, like wrist bands, except they go on your arms," says Natasha Kai. "I wear pink and white ones. I feel like I have to have something on my arms. Also, every year I choose a different hair style, for luck. The strangest one was when I had my hair really short and I spiked it. It was long in front, spiked in the back with gel. Man, never again would I do that."

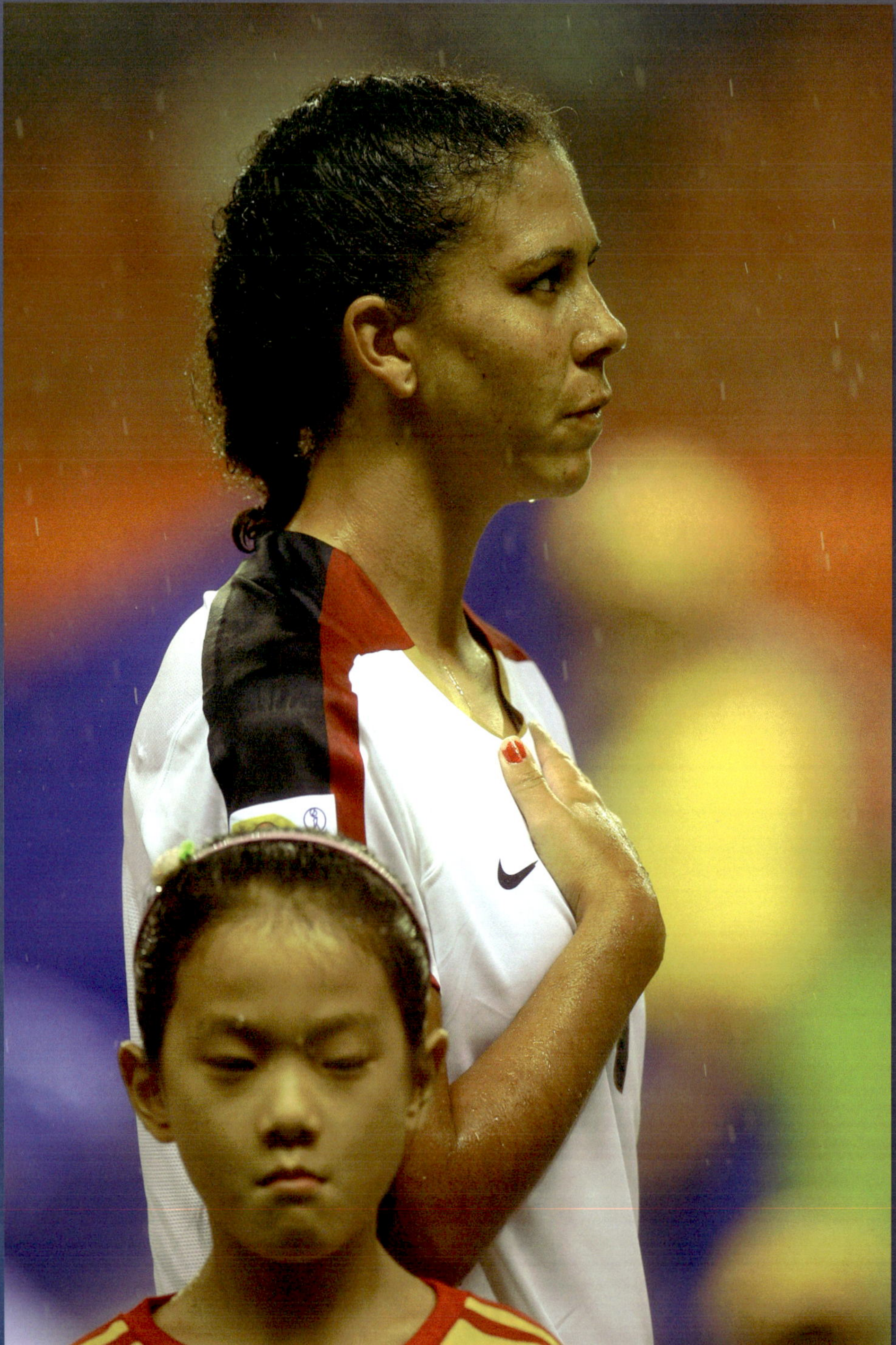

Oh, man, that was such a relief to me! So I worked for a year, and took time off from soccer. Not once did I play. I played every other sport—basketball, volleyball, you name it. Just hung out, didn't think about soccer."

When she went to college the next year, she says she felt completely relaxed. "It was fun again," she says. "That break was like a breath of fresh air for me. And luckily, I'd been active, so my game hadn't lost anything. I was in shape. So it ended up great—but it wouldn't have, I don't think, if I'd been forced to go to college right away."

Falling Out of Love

For Shannon Boxx, it felt like she had fallen out of love with the game of soccer—unexpectedly. After a successful soccer career in college, she played in a semi-professional league in Germany.

"I went on my own," she says. "I thought it would be a great experience, and I was very confident. But that didn't last long. It was a really different style of game, and I went from playing all the time, to not playing at all. I never knew why—it seemed like there was no reason. I didn't like the coach, it just wasn't fun anymore. I mean, I'd been training, playing, doing all this stuff, and I got to Germany and forgot the game could be fun. It just wasn't."

Boxx went home and started thinking about what her career should be. Soccer, she said, was no longer an option. "I hung up my boots," she says. And it might have ended there if she hadn't gotten a call from a friend inviting her to play in a soccer game.

Team warms up as rain from Typhoon Wipha begins to fall before the Nigeria game.

Shannon Boxx and Chinese youth partner put up with rain during the National Anthem.

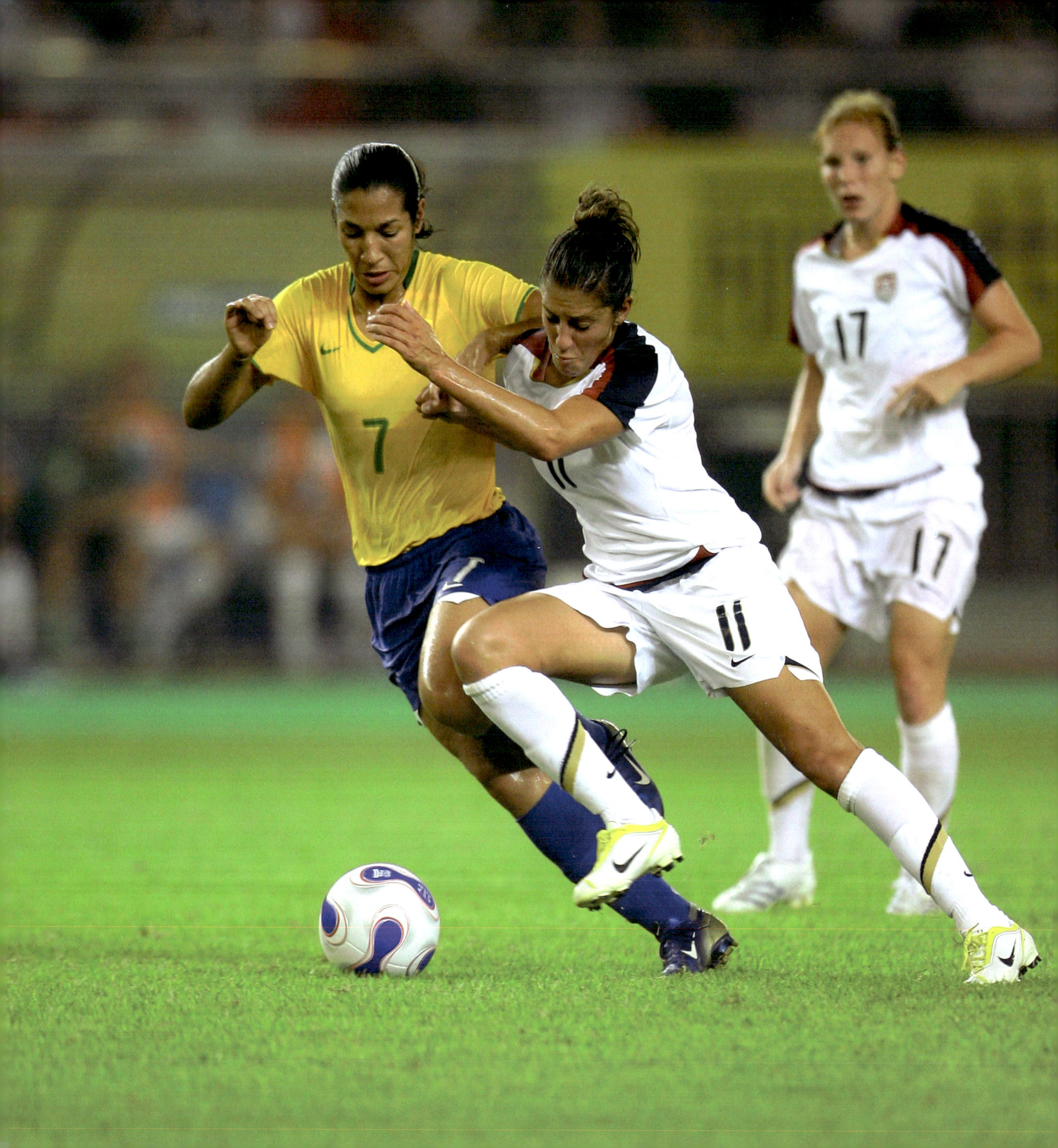

"I told her I was done with soccer. But she convinced me—she said it was just a fun league, all girls, and they really needed a player. So I went, and I loved it. I had the best time of my life. I learned to love the game of soccer all over again. There was no pressure, no worrying about making mistakes. So I kept playing in that league. And I realized how much I'd missed it. And when the WUSA [Women's United Soccer Association] started, I thought, I want to do that. I want to play."

"Coaches Have So Much Power"

Carli Lloyd says that the problem is frequently a coach who forgets—or perhaps never knew—how much power he or she can have over a player's self-esteem. "If you have a coach who puts you down and says you're not good, or you lack talent, that makes it so hard. It doesn't matter if it's recreational league or Division-I college soccer."

Boxx agrees wholeheartedly. "It's really hard when a coach doesn't communicate. Too many coaches just bench you, without telling you why. And that makes no sense at all. That's happened to most players, I'm sure. You go from playing a lot to playing five minutes or less. And you get to thinking, is it me? Am I not a good player anymore? Am I not as good as I thought I was? What did I do wrong?"

Lloyd says that she has gradually learned that if she continues to play, it is important to accept the fact that soccer can be a roller coaster. "I can control how hard I train," she says. "I can control how I play, how unselfish I can be as a player, and how good and supportive a teammate I can be. But I

Lloyd drives to the goal in Chicago.

Carli Lloyd beats Brazil's Daniela to win the ball.

Leslie Osborne works on her foot skills during practice.

can't control my coach. I can't control whether I start, or how much time I play. Knowing the difference between what I can control and what I can't makes a big difference in how I feel."

"The Worst Five Months"

Getting cut from a team is a particularly humbling experience, and Leslie Osborne can still remember how miserable she felt when it happened to her. "I was the second one cut from the Olympic team in 2004," she says. "I had the worst five months I've had in soccer. I was awful in the residency camp with those girls. I was miserable and lonely—I was away from home, from my family, my college team, my boyfriend. When you feel miserable, you can't play well. It really affected me, really diminished my confidence.

"I came back to college, not sure if I ever wanted to play soccer again. I felt like a failure. It was my college coach, Jerry Smith, who talked to me, let me cry about it. He was patient and supportive, and said the things I needed to hear, I guess.

"But that whole experience made me realize how easy it is to be defined by other people. And somehow, because of getting cut, I had started defining myself as a failure—and that was a dangerous thing. Thank goodness for Jerry Smith."

Osborne gets water during a stoppage against Sweden.

Christie Rampone soars over a North Korean player.

Kristine Lilly collides with a Swedish defender while attempting a header.

Physical Challenges

Injuries are another part of the game. Players have all had injuries. Some take months to heal, others heal more quickly. But all injuries present special challenges to players who want to see less of the bench, and more of the field.

There is no good time for an injury, says Christie Rampone, but there are definitely times that are worse than others. She suffered a concussion during the third-place match against Norway in the World Cup. "I went up for a header," she says, "and got into a three-way collision. The goalie got a little of me. That thing happens all the time, with no serious consequences, but this time, it just hit me in the wrong spot.

"I lost vision in my right eye. I thought, okay. I'll come through this—I just got knocked, and it'll come back. No big deal. The thing is, I didn't lose consciousness. Just vision. I was blurry and tried to fight through it. There was about five minutes left in the first half. I mean, I didn't want to leave the field—it was such an important game. I did not understand that you don't fight through a concussion."

"Everything Was Kind of Going in Slow Motion"

Rampone says that she told her defenders right away what had happened. "They knew—I was talking to them," she says. "I said, 'I got hit and I'm okay, just blurry.' But then at halftime, it hit me hard. I went into the locker room and it got worse. I told the coach I wanted to go back out, that he should give me five minutes, and let's see if it clears up. Then I stepped on the field and I couldn't focus on the ball. Not at all. Everything was kind of going in slow motion, and I realized I couldn't do it."

Banana Pancakes

Some players admit they are superstitious about certain activities before a game—that they play better when those things take place. For Shannon Boxx, eating a particular type of breakfast is a must. "Banana pancakes," she says simply. "I go by myself down to the restaurant and order banana pancakes and coffee. Everyone on the team knows that I do that. I've been doing that since college. Actually, I wasn't sure I'd be able to find them in China, but I did. I just got regular pancakes, and cut up a banana on there, and I was good."

"

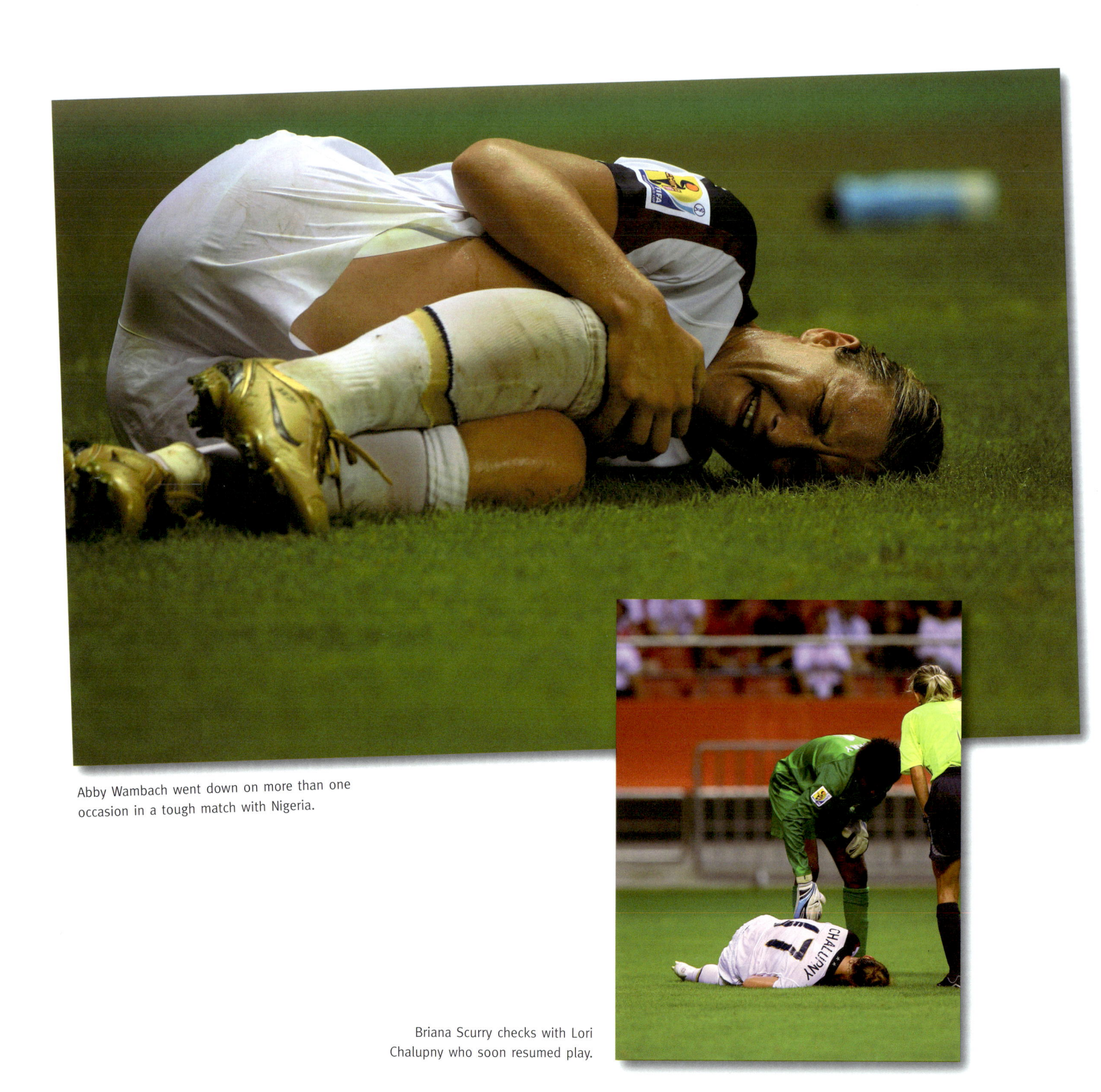

Abby Wambach went down on more than one occasion in a tough match with Nigeria.

Briana Scurry checks with Lori Chalupny who soon resumed play.

She ended up going to the hospital, and is grateful she did. "I had been in the locker room, and I thought maybe I was feeling a little better. So I started going back out to watch the game. And then I relapsed, so they took me to the hospital. I didn't have any sense of where I was, and all I wanted to do was to go to sleep. I still feel cheated a little, not having any closure about that World Cup. I didn't see it, didn't have the memory of it."

"A Hard, Hard Year"

In some cases, though the injury isn't as dramatic, it is more severe and thus takes longer to heal. Aly Wagner did not get to play in the World Cup until the very last game because of a groin injury that plagued her through most of 2007. She admits she was very frustrated at sitting on the bench during the tournament.

"I came in with an injury, and I knew I wouldn't be able to play ninety minutes each game," she says. "I knew [the coaches] were being conservative with me. But it was so hard. I think I could have contributed something in each of the games, but it's ultimately a coach's decision. But you know, you dedicate a whole year to something and not have it happen, it's just frustrating. It shows you again what you can't control. But as hard as it was sitting those first games, it was really nice to play in the third place game."

Shannon Boxx knows the feeling of finally coming back after an injury. "I had a lot of surgeries in one year, from August 2006 to August 2007," she explains. "It was a left knee thing, then a right knee thing, then my right hip. Surgery, lots and lots of rehab, and all the emotional ups and downs that go

The team played short for nine minutes against North Korea while Abby Wambach was getting stitches in the back of her head. She received two during the game, eleven more after—all without pain killers.

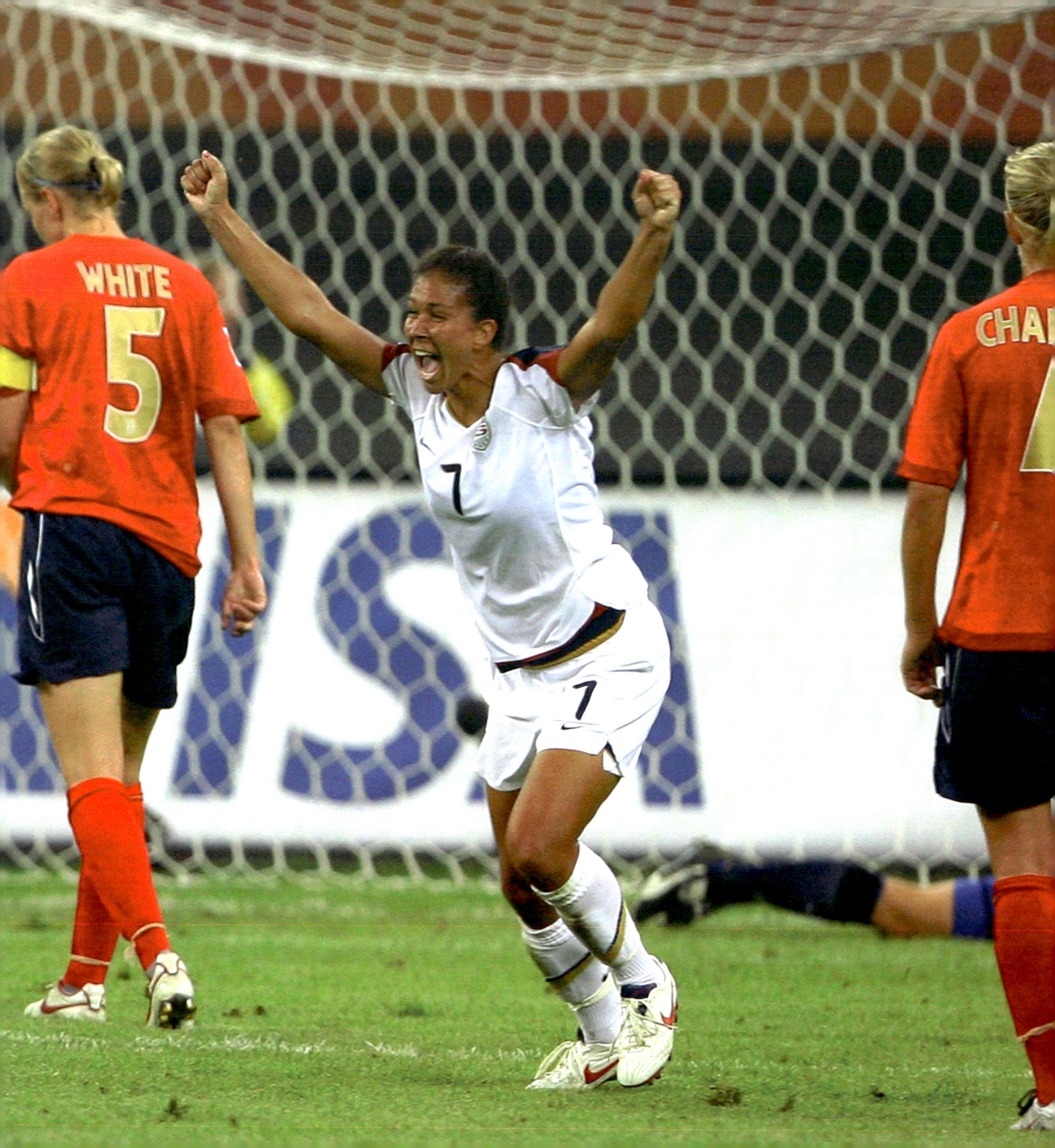
WHITE
5
7

with something like that. And my team was always there for me, being supportive. That meant a lot.

"So anyway, it was funny—during the game with England, I scored a goal, and I was so happy. But if you look at the video, my face just broke into tears as I ran into Abby and Leslie's arms. Afterwards, I'm like, 'Why did I do that?' But I realized that it had been such a hard, hard year. I didn't realize how hard until I was back, I guess."

"Not Everybody Starts"

Whether biding time because of an injury or just waiting for an opportunity to play, every player has spent time on the bench. Surprisingly, however, the players on this team say that those on the bench at any one time are valuable, too.

"The thing is, not everybody starts," says Briana Scurry. "It sounds obvious, but on a team like this one, you've got the best players from the best teams in the United States. None of us spent too much time on the bench during college, unless maybe it was for an injury. At this level, on this team, everybody is good enough to be a starter, but there's only eleven on the field at one time.

"I don't like sitting on the bench," she continues. "Nobody does. It's hard. I'm a competitor, and I want to play all the time. That's natural. But I've got to tell you honestly, when I was on the bench, I was behind my teammates the whole time. I take pride in my role, even on the bench, to support my team."

Shannon Boxx accepts congratulations from Christie Rampone and Cat Whitehill.

Shannon Boxx is jubilant after scoring a goal against England.

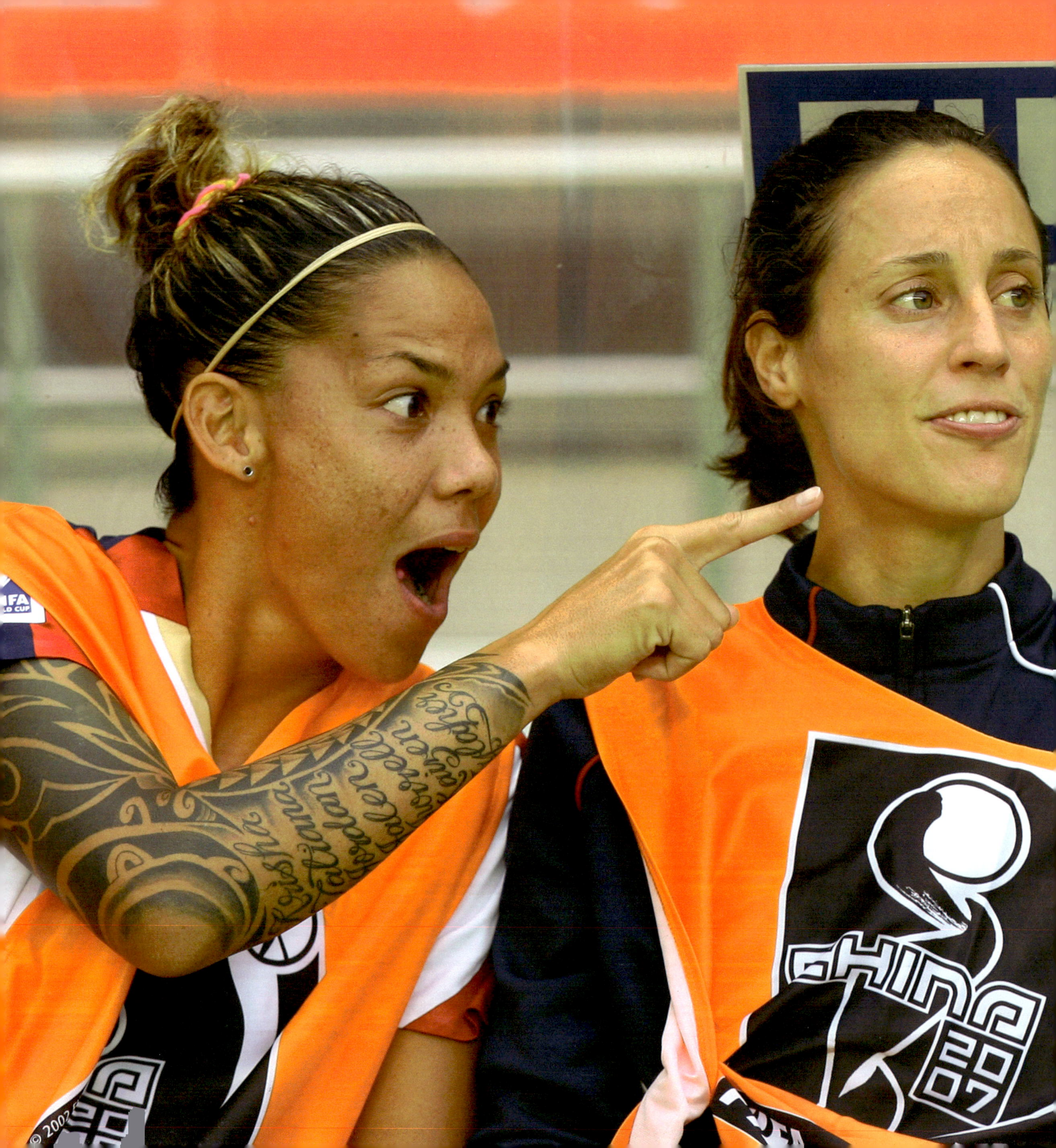
CHINA
2007

As the third goalie, Nicole Barnhart says she has spent a lot of time on the bench. "But we make an impact," she insists. "We always yell encouragement as much as we can. Players come off the field and say, 'Thanks you guys—we can hear you. Keep it up, it helps us.' I'd love to be playing, but I'm proud of being on this team. Really, every time I put on the U.S. jersey, I feel proud that we're representing our country. And I know I'll get my chance."

From left to right: Angela Hucles, Leslie Osborne, Marci (Jobson) Miller, Tina Ellertson

Natash Kai, to the left of Kate Markgraf, is momentarily distracted.

From left to right: Shannon Boxx, Kristine Lilly, Marian Dalmy, Hucles, Markgraf, Heather O'Reilly and Nicole Barnhart are entertained by Kai's play on the field.

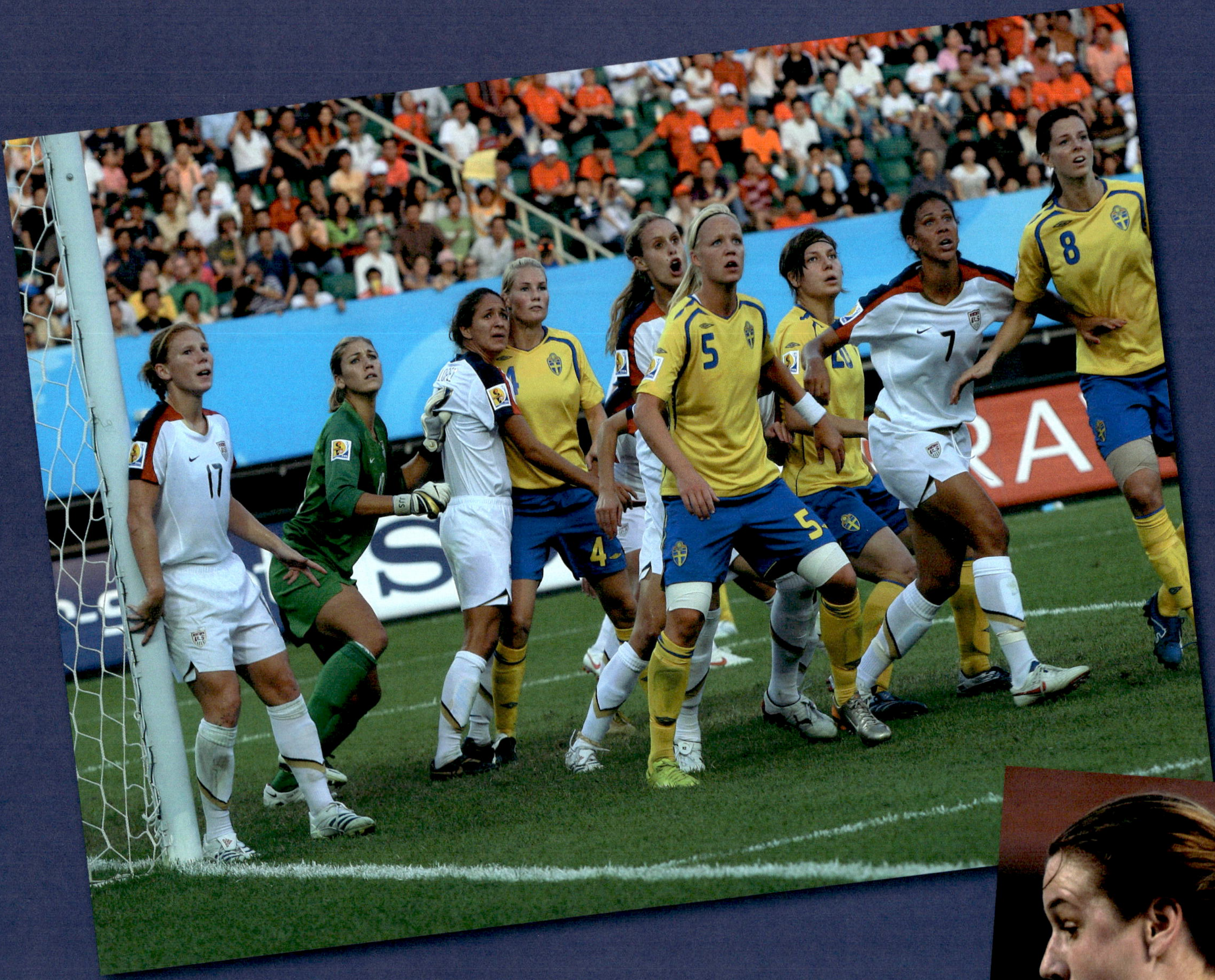

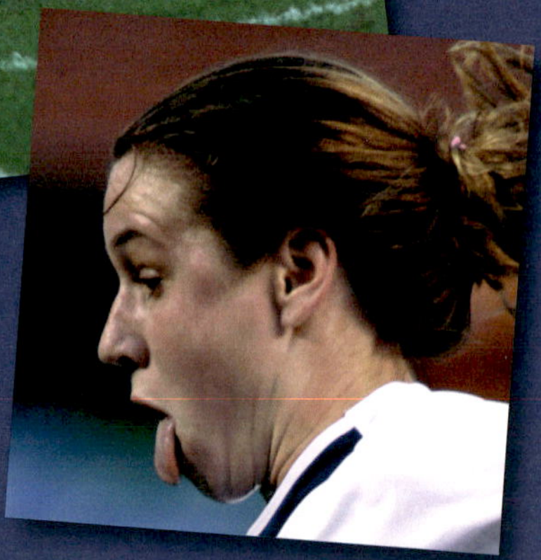

chapter 5

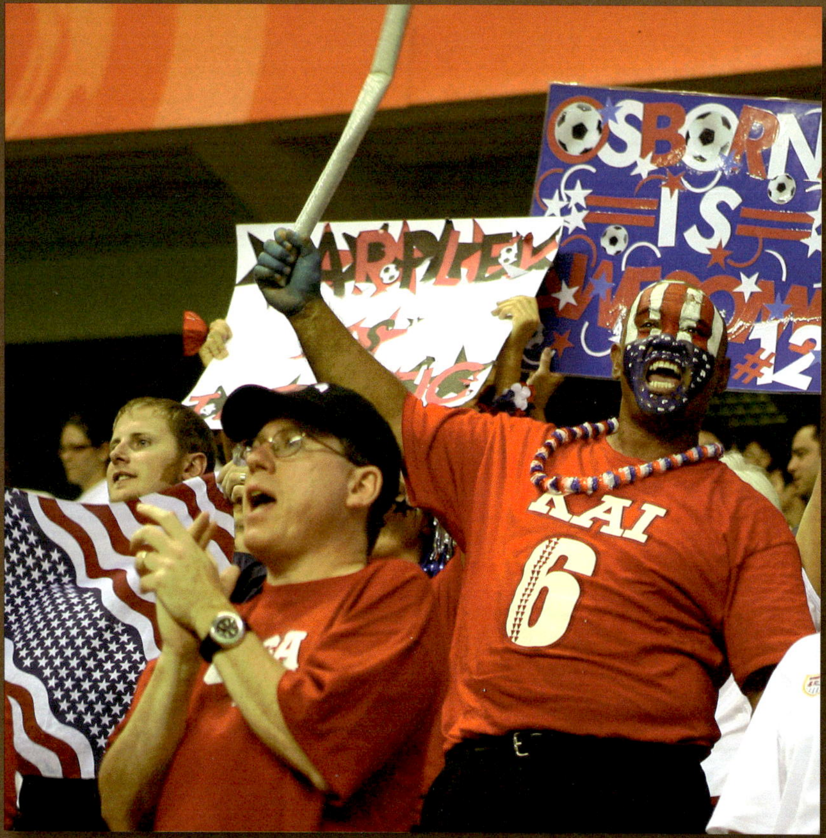
OSBORN
IS
#12

do overs

Though they hold different opinions on many topics, the women on this team are unanimous in their pleasure at how their lives have turned out. They are successful, skilled soccer players and they have contributed mightily to the nation's top women's soccer team. They have had the support of loving families, friends, and fans, and have been able to travel the world representing their country.

That said, however, most of the players admit that they would do some things differently if given a chance. Years of experience playing at the highest levels of soccer have taught them many lessons. And they want to share these experiences with younger players.

"I'd Be More Careful With My Words"

Some of the lessons they've learned go beyond the playing field. "If I could go back to being twelve, the first thing that comes to mind is how I'd treat people," says Cat Whitehill. "You know, that's the thing as you get older—you think about whether you treated people right—classmates, friends, whatever. When you're that age, you don't think that much about it. I hope I did, but I'm not sure.

"To me it's kind of a scary thought. I mean, what if I said something mean or flippant to someone and it really made a bad difference in their life?

Cat Whitehill

Natasha Kai's father Benny wears his game face.

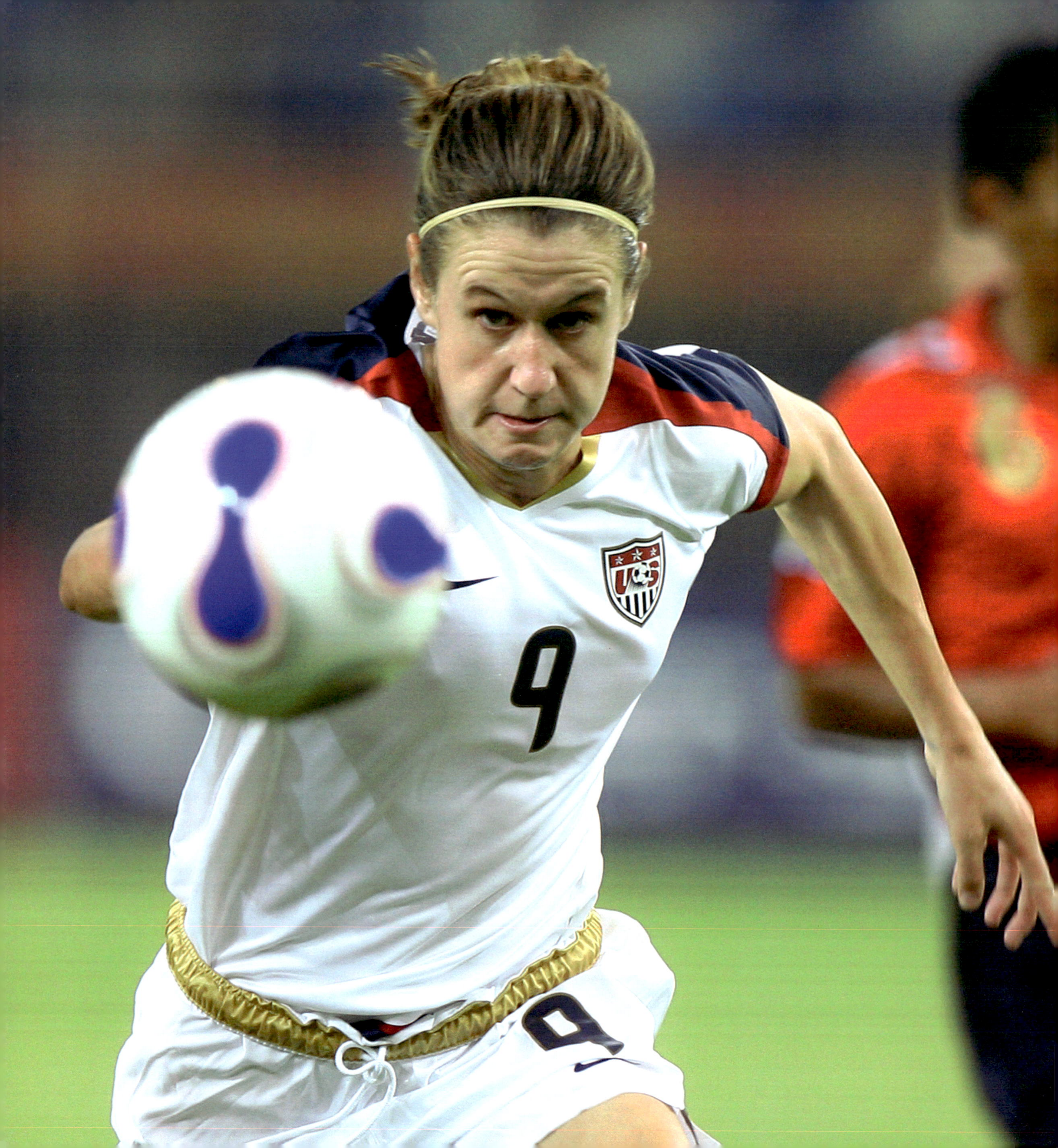

I don't remember doing anything like that, but I just hope I didn't. You know, on a bad day, you don't always realize the impact your words can have. As I get older, I realize it, because I think about the times people's words have had an impact on me. So, I guess I'd be more careful with my words."

Christie Rampone would have changed her words, too—not in the type, but the number she'd use. "Like I said before, I was always really shy. And sometimes that's okay. But the thing is, when you're on a team like this, it's important for all of our voices to be heard. When there's an issue to be discussed—whatever it is—I still tend to sit back and read people, get the tempo of the team, but not voice my ideas. I'd think things, but I wouldn't say them. I wish I'd learned how to do that when I was younger."

"It Would Be an Expensive Present, But a Great One"

For most of the team, however, the biggest do-overs from their youth would relate to soccer. "What I would have done, if I could go back to being a kid, is to spend more time with the ball," says Heather O'Reilly. "I'd ask for a ball bag for my twelfth birthday—one of those big bags coaches carry with all the team balls. And five or six balls to put in there. It would be an expensive present," she says, thinking about it. "But a great one. Maybe it would be combination birthday and Christmas present or something. But then I'd have no excuse not to train.

Christie Rampone was named Captain of the 2008 WNT squad.

It's easy to see the passion Heather O'Reilly has for the game.

Stephanie (Lopez) Cox and teammates getting ready for a practice session

"See, when I was younger, I'd find all kinds of excuses not to train—especially in the winter. But if a player is serious about wanting to grow up and get to the highest levels of soccer, she or he has to spend time on the ball. It's all about being comfortable with both feet, shooting from all different angles. I used to kick against a wall, but if I'd had that ball bag and all those balls, I would have gone to the park and spent an hour shooting and doing ball work. With one ball, it's a drag, because you have to keep retrieving it.

"And," she says, warming up to the scenario, "I'd get myself a training partner. I'd suggest to anyone reading this, a young player, I'd tell them to get a friend, someone you can call up on the spur of the moment and just say, let's go train. On the youth soccer level, you don't train more than two or three times a week, and that's not enough for a serious player. The thing is, even if you don't have a partner, you could take that ball bag and you wouldn't have any excuses not to get out there and work. Seven hours a week, you'd see amazing results. I would do that, if I could go back to being twelve."

"Even When No One's Looking"

Many of the players express remorse that they had not understood the value of training and conditioning when they were younger. "When you're a kid, that's boring," says Angela Hucles. "It's more fun to play games or practice shooting. When you're a young player, you don't get how hard you really have to work on the other stuff, even when no one's looking. I wish I had known that earlier. When you get older, you realize how much better you could be if only you'd worked harder on those things earlier.

Lori Chalupny

Marci (Jobson) Miller

Cat Whitehill

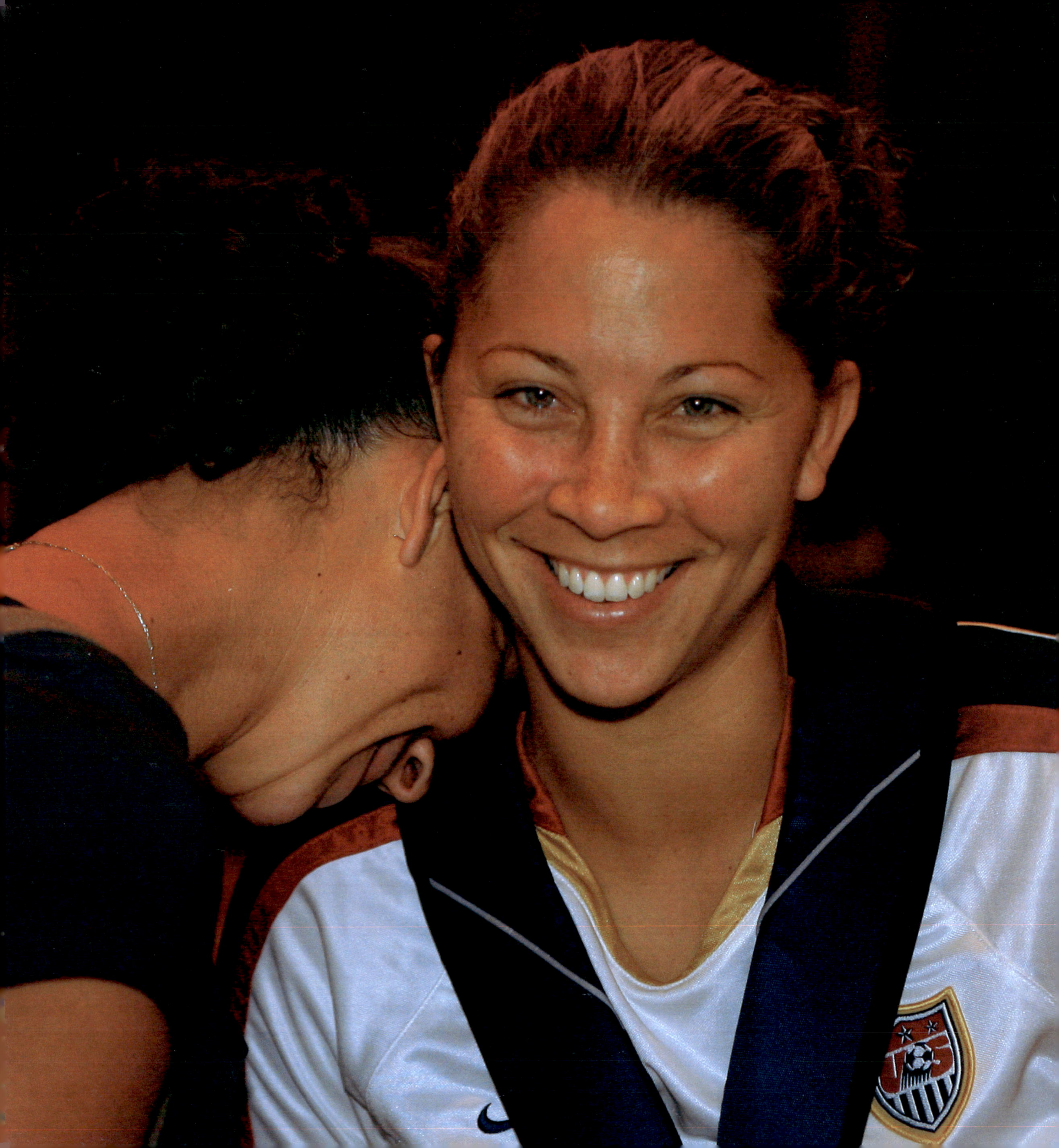

"I really believe that, too," says Shannon Boxx. "When I was younger, I didn't realize what being in shape really meant. I used to train, and I'd think, 'Great, I'm fit.' But then I'd go up against someone like Kristine Lilly, and I'm like, 'Well, okay, I guess I'm not fit at all.'"

Boxx did the minimum amount of conditioning—just enough to get by, she says. "I know that for someone reading this maybe it doesn't make sense. But really, as you get to each level, the level of fitness needed to succeed increases, too. And if you aren't prepared you won't be able to perform on that higher level."

A Matter of Survival

Boxx says her whole life changed after she got traded from the WSA team she had been playing on. "I'd been playing for a WSA team, the San Diego Spirit, for two years. It was great—I'm from California, so it meant playing close to home, having my friends and family see me play. It was great for the first season and a half. But then—remember what I told you about what happened in Germany? How I went and the coach there never let me play? Well, in San Diego, they changed coaches midway through my first year, and he changed things. I went from playing the whole game to getting in maybe five minutes. So there I was again, losing confidence again, just like after Germany."

After that second season, she was traded to the New York Power. She felt rejected, as though she had failed. "That's when I hired a friend of mine to be my personal trainer," she says. "And it changed everything. See, I needed to have someone be there while I trained, because I didn't know how to do it on

Boxx warms up in rain.

Shannon Boxx enjoys a moment with her sister Gillian Boxx, who won a softball Gold Medal at the 1996 Olympics.

Lindsay Tarpley freezes her New Zealand defender with a nice cut.

my own. I didn't know how to push myself. If I'm by myself, I get tired and say, 'Okay, that's good enough.' But that wasn't getting it done."

Boxx says that young players would be wise to learn about training early, because the benefits are huge. "I needed [my trainer] to push me, to tell me to keep going. Your body gets tired, but you really never know what your limit is, you know? Until you push yourself. And you do that when you're doing a drill or an exercise, by doing just one more than what they asked for. Like if you have to do ten sprints, do eleven. Then the next time, do twelve, and so on. Do more in your training than you do in a game. Do more than you'll ever be asked to do on a team fitness test. Then you really know you're ready." The hard work enabled Boxx to succeed on her New York team, and eventually powered her to a spot on the National Team.

Angela Hucles says there's another reason to really learn how to train. "Away from the team, you don't have access to the team's facilities," she explains. "So you have to have your own exercise routines, your own way to keep fit—running, strength training, all of that stuff. If you're serious about soccer, you have to be serious about training. You can't fake being fit, that's for sure. But it really makes a difference when you are in shape and ready. Not only physically, but confidence-wise, too. It's empowering."

"Look at it this way," says Abby Wambach. "If it were easy, everyone would do it. And they really don't. It's not easy at all. It's maybe the hardest thing about being a soccer player. The good players spend years doing the training to get to this level. It's the mental discipline, like Boxxy says. But if you think you want to play someday at this level, you've got to do it. For me, the day I can't mentally get myself to train hard—that's the day I retire."

Taking a Step Back

"Sometimes I like to take a step back and appreciate where I am, what experiences I've had," says Angela Hucles. "I love that, realizing how awesome it is to be part of this team. I'm proud, and I feel humbled by it. I wish everyone could experience how great this feels."

Angela Hucles

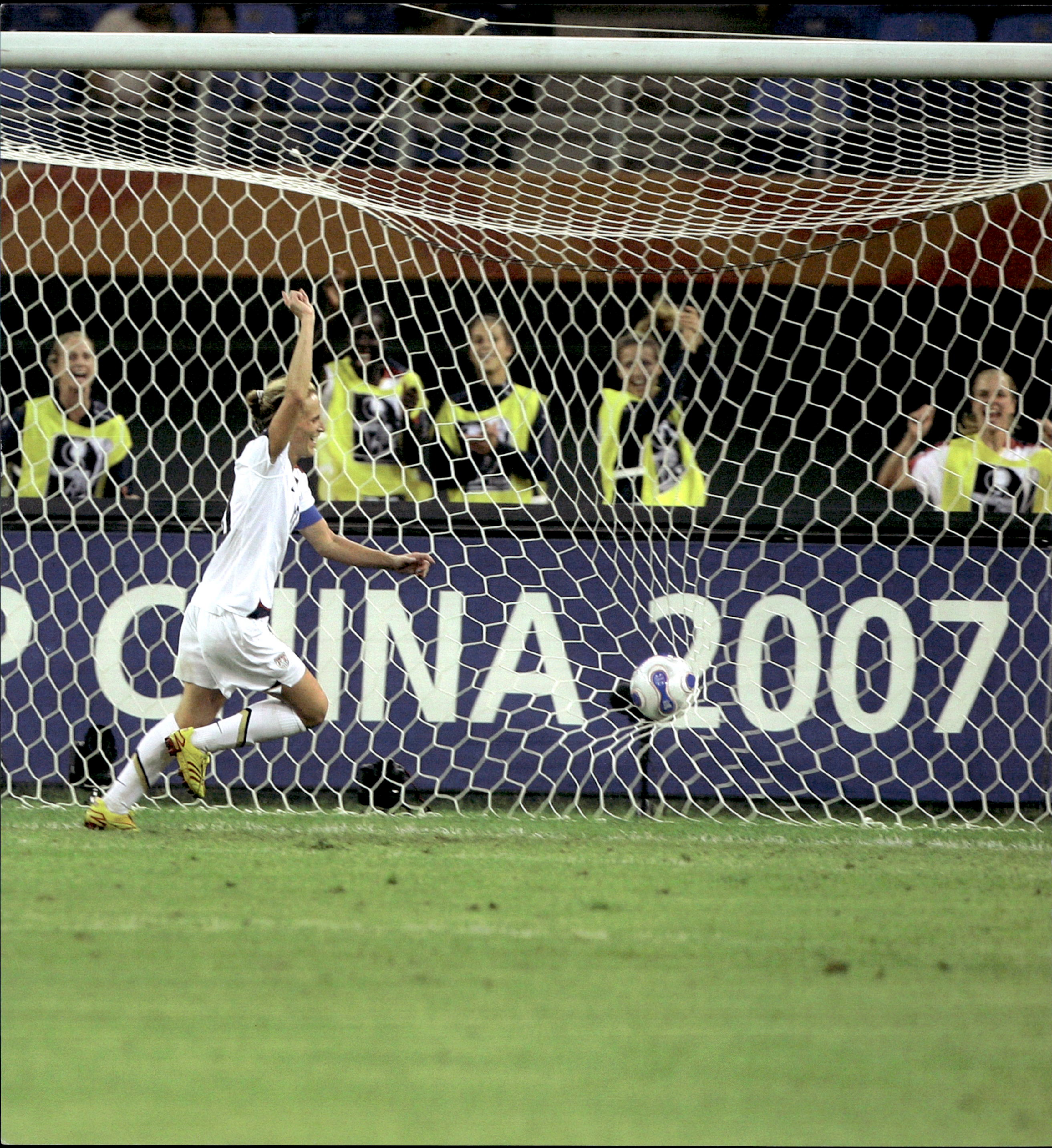

HINA 2007

Speaking of Retiring....

At first it seems hard to imagine any of these players not playing. But there will come a day when each of them decides to make a life after soccer. Asked what sort of life that will be, some admit they're not sure. Maybe they'll open a business, maybe they'll marry and have families. They just don't know.

Others have some ideas that fire them up. "I want to hike the Appalachian Trail," says Abby Wambach. "Maybe do more work with Right to Play. I like the idea of traveling—seeing new things. But how to earn a living, I'm not sure."

Aly Wagner has some practical ideas. "I've always been interested in money, like the stock market. That intrigues me. I think business is in my future. Maybe advertising or marketing. I come up with ads in my head a lot—maybe I could try to do that for a living."

Marian Dalmy is on that same page. "I majored in communications in college. My dream job has been to work for Nike—marketing some of their products. Like, if they came out with a new shoe or something, I'd like to come up with strategies to market it and get it out there. That sounds challenging and fun to me."

"Soccer Is What I've Always Done"

Many of the players say that whatever career path they choose, it will somehow include soccer. "It would be very hard not to be involved in soccer," says Leslie Osborne. "I can think about having kids, and having another kind of life, but soccer is what I've always done. Somehow, on some level, I kind of

Abby Wambach had six goals in the 2007 World Cup, second highest, winning the Silver Shoe Award.

Kristine Lilly scores against England, her 129th international goal, as Marci (Jobson) Miller, Tina Ellertson, Carli Lloyd, Aly Wagner and Lindsay Tarpley cheer from the warm-up area.

Things We'd Change If We Could

Kristine Lilly I'd wear more dresses. I like wearing them now, but when I was a girl, I hated dressing up, just hated it.

Carli Lloyd I think I would have tried to not let people hurt my feelings or offend me. I'd get down on myself if someone made a comment to me. It's so hard being twelve.

Aly Wagner I'd have taken piano lessons. I took some, but didn't embrace it at all. I hated practicing, so I don't remember any of it now. But I'd love to be able to sit down, unwind, and play like I've seen my mom do.

Aly Wagner doing "left hand only."

think I'll be doing something related to the game. Broadcasting, maybe—I'd love to try that."

Broadcasting sounds fun to Cat Whitehill, too, but she's got far more specific goals, including the network where she'd work. "For a long time, I've wanted to be on ESPN College Gameday," she says. "I absolutely love college football—remember, I'm from the South, so that speaks for itself—and the idea of being a football reporter is exciting. So that's my goal, after soccer is done."

Kristine Lilly, who has played on the team longer than anyone, says she is probably closest to making those decisions. "I agree with Ozzy about staying connected to soccer. I'd like to maybe coach. But one other thing that really interests me is the Special Olympics. I've been involved for about three years on the state level in Connecticut with intellectually disabled adults. The people I've worked with really have a great time. It's rewarding giving these athletes a way to compete. And it's refreshing to watch people playing who have no pretenses at all. It's pure fun. So maybe I'd do more with the Special Olympics after I'm done playing."

Kristine Lilly relaxes in the team's Tianjin hotel lobby.

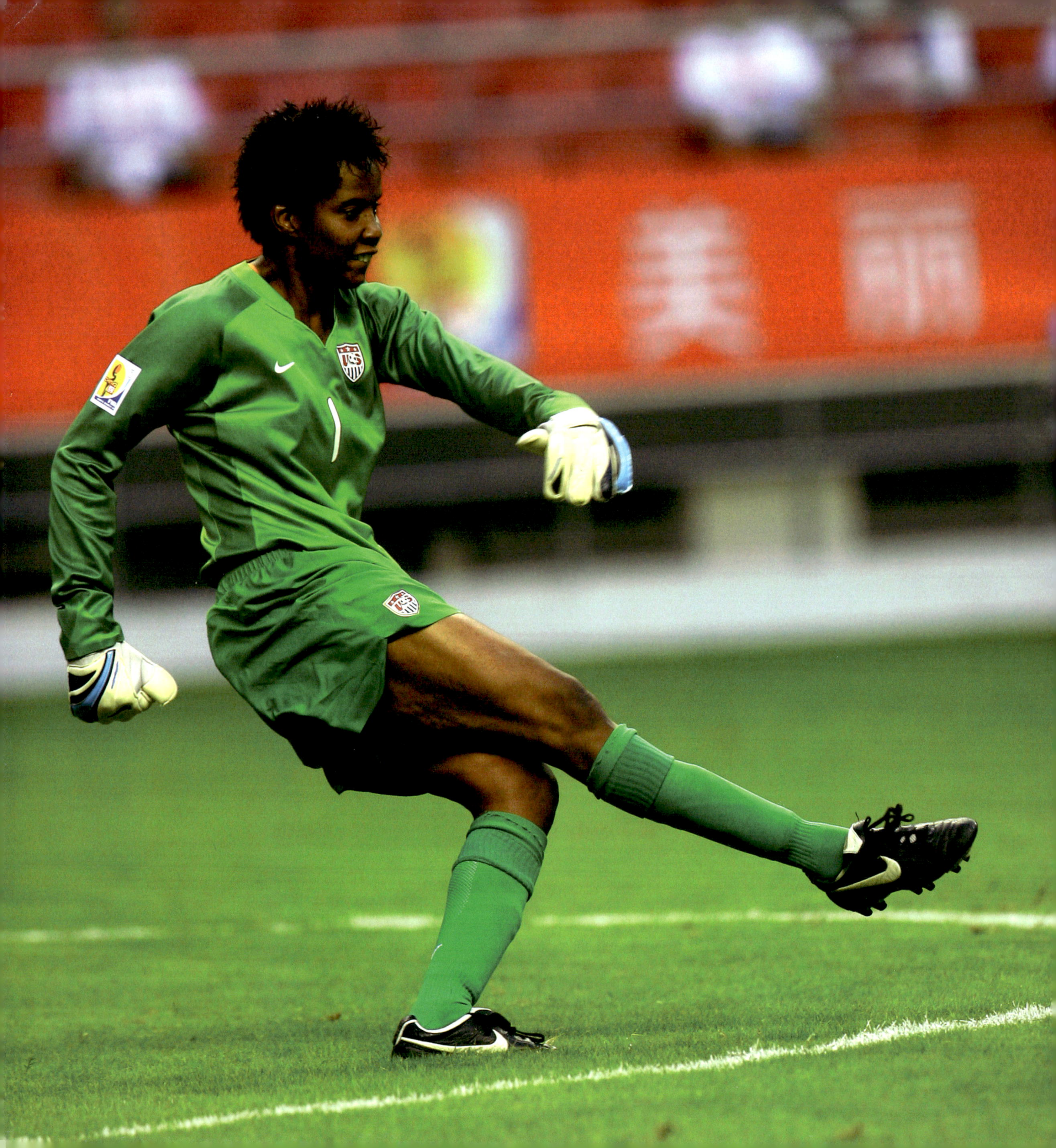
美丽

"It's Been a Dream of Mine"

Interestingly, many of the players do not have aspirations for a career in whatever they studied in college. "I was a political science major, with an economics minor," says Briana Scurry. "When I was in college, I was thinking about being a lawyer—that was my goal. But now, that doesn't seem likely. After playing soccer for so long, the idea of going back to a classroom for three years of law school doesn't seem too appealing right now. And I don't think I want to stay in soccer after playing."

Her idea now, she says, has far more appeal than law. "I want to be in development, designing facilities for the elderly." She says that her idea stems in large part from her experiences with her father, who was very ill for years before his death. "I want to design something that's way better than what my dad had. So many of the facilities now have elderly people just shut off from life, from young people. I'd change that."

Her idea, she says, is to make residents feel needed. "I want all seniors who are living in my facility to feel that they're still contributing to society. Too many seniors now don't feel they have value, that nothing they know or do has purpose. If they feel valuable, I think they'll have a happier life. I'm going to have a youth component, where kids come in and share ideas with seniors. I'd love to see an eighty-year-old man playing Xbox with a fifteen-year-old girl, and talking, having fun. In the process, they'd be learning a little bit about each other's culture. It's a big dream—pretty titanic," she admits. "But what a great outcome it could have, right?"

Scurry plows through Norway player to stop a play.

Briana Scurry shows great form with goal kick.

Natasha Kai has one-on-one conversation with Lindsay Tarpley during stretching exercises.

"I Wasn't the Straightest Kid, Either"

For Natasha Kai, the future might include going back to school. "I didn't finish," she says. "Soccer kind of interrupted that. I was a sociology major. My goal is in some way to work with troubled kids. Hawaii isn't any different from anywhere else—there's lots of kids that are having trouble finding their way. They come from families that aren't privileged, and they're struggling. I maybe could help give them some help."

She laughs. "Hey, I wasn't the straightest kid, either. I got into trouble when I was growing up. If I came back, knowing what I know, having been through what I have, I maybe could help."

The other idea she toys with is being a police officer. "I think about that, too," she says. "There's a lot of police officers who have their belts a little too tight, if you know what I mean. It's maybe too much of a power thing, and they can't relate. But I'm a people person. I think I could be one of those police officers who can talk to people without being scary. Either way, I want to help. I've been lucky in my life, my family. And, after soccer, it'll be time to give back."

Kai always has something going, even when she's doing nothing.

" a link in the chain "

"Words can't explain what it feels like to be on this team," says Natasha Kai. "They're my family away from home. They're all my sisters. I'm so honored to be part of them. We are together, working like a family, trying so hard to fight on the soccer field for our country. And the part I'm proudest of is that we're opening doors for the younger girls that are coming up, so they have it better than we did. Mia Hamm, Michelle Akers, Julie Foudy—they did that for us. And we're a link in the chain, doing it for the next generation."

"I Miss These Guys"

No matter how exciting their dreams may be for after soccer, the players agree on one more thing—that they are going to cherish every minute on this team for however long they play. "It's kind of funny, says Shannon Boxx. "I mean, we travel together, spend like twenty-four hours a day together when we're on the road. But then you come home and you have a break, and it feels strange. Like after China, we were apart for ten days. And by the end of that time, I was so excited to see them all again—like it had been months! That cracks me up."

They all realize they are not guaranteed a position on the team. They know that younger players will replace them someday. And that's the way it's supposed to be. "That is the thing about this team," says Angela Hucles. "It's bigger than any of us. We'll all eventually get replaced—even the greatest players. But the tradition of the team will go on, and we'll always be a part of it. That makes me really, really proud."

Abby Wambach wished she could have a do-over after missing a shot against Nigeria.

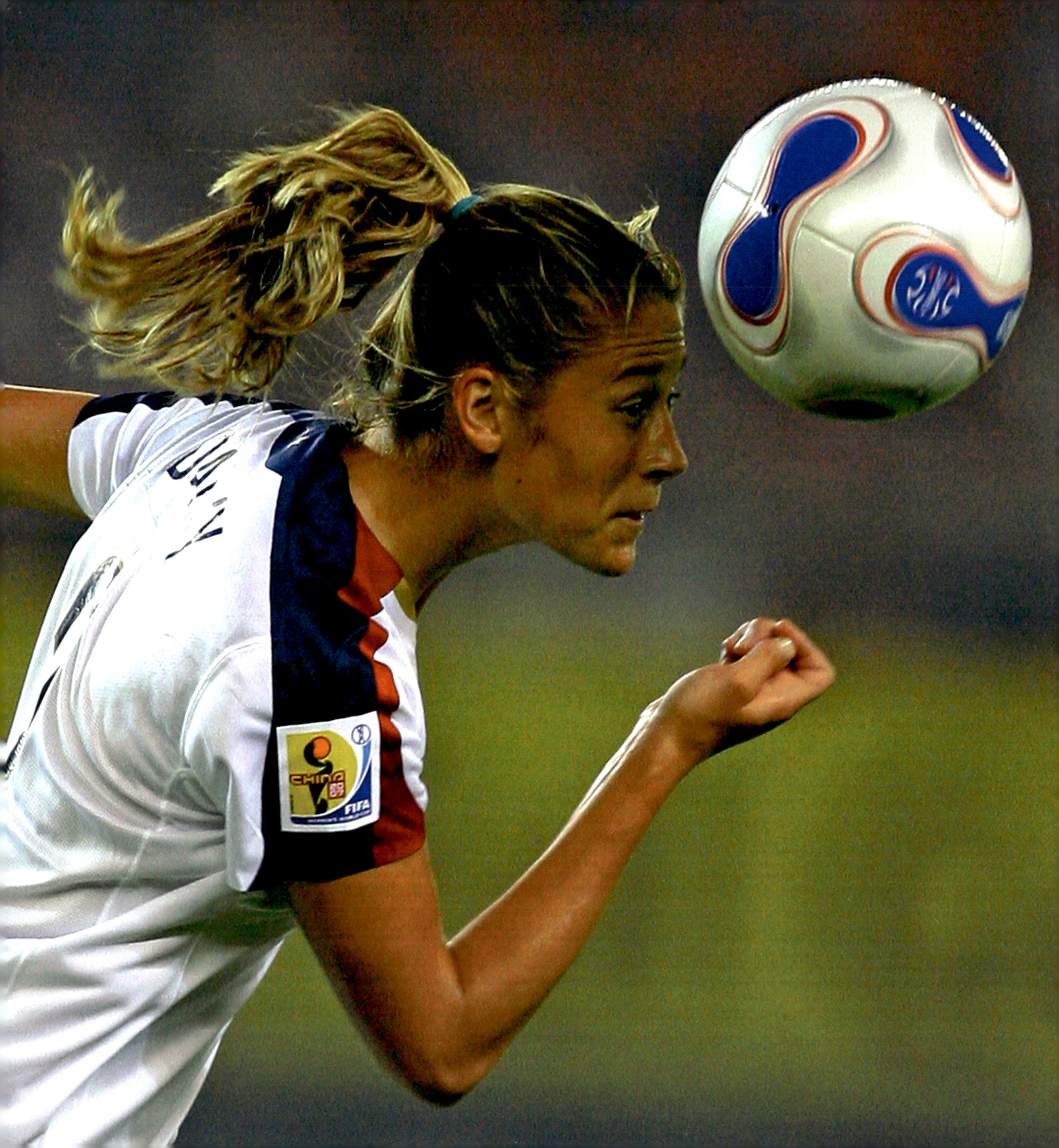
CHINA
FIFA

thank you

With thanks to friends, family, players and business associates who helped make this book possible: to Paul Phillips who spawned the idea for this project and followed the team for thousands of miles to capture pictures; to Gail Stewart for her love of the game and ability to write simply and with clarity for all readers; to Julie Foudy for lending us her good name and insight; to Steve Loop for his daily sunshine and penchant for lists; to Carl Franzén for art direction, marketing jabs and one song; to Diane Cassidy whose friendship and support have been indispensable; to Kristine Smith for wisdom; to Jonathan Phillips for technical expertise; to the geeks at August Ash for a cool portraitofpassion.com; to our thousands of MySpace friends; to Dillon Bersten and Schwann's USA Cup for the use of the Julie Foudy photo on page 5; to the player's families for sharing pictures of their daughters; to Andy and Carol O'Reilly for Heather's shoes; and especially to current and past players who, through the Women's National Team Players' Association, support this effort. Go USA!

Kristine Lilly

Christie Rampone

Marian Dalmy

Marci (Jobson) Miller

Lindsay Tarpley

Tina Ellertson

Stephanie (Lopez) Cox

Abby Wambach

Briana Scurry

Heather O'Reilly and Leslie Osborne

Aly Wagner

Angela Hucles

Hope Solo

Lori Chalupny

Cat Whitehill

Natasha Kai

Carli Lloyd

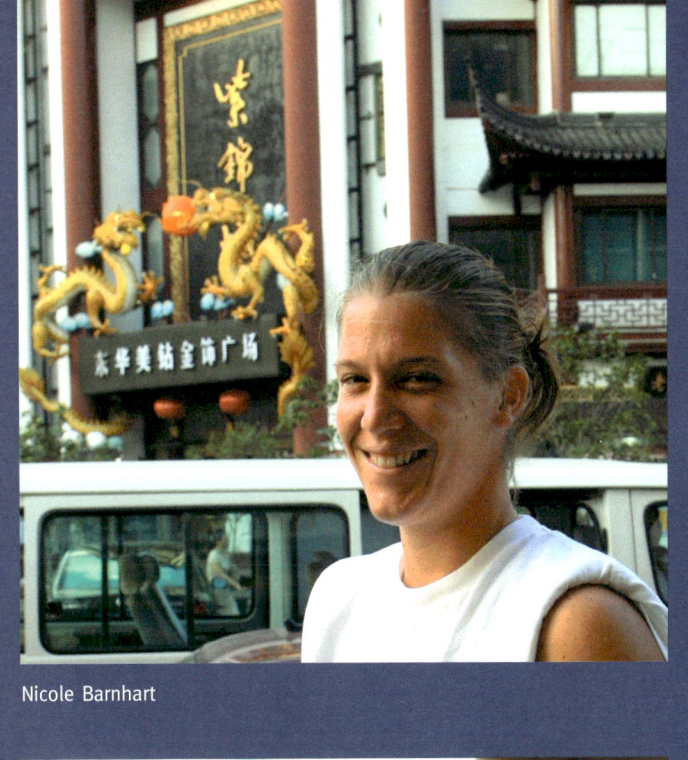

Nicole Barnhart

Shannon Boxx

Kate Markgraf

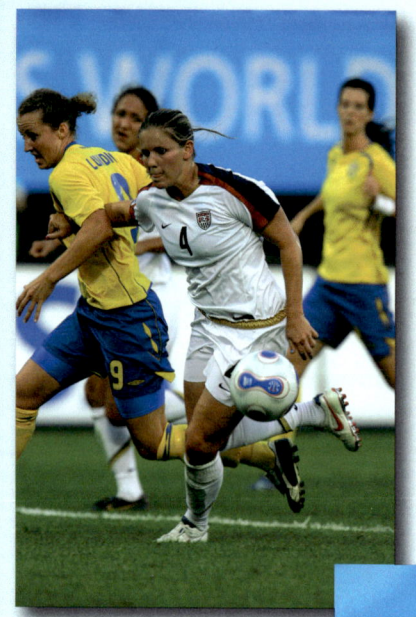

Two Furious Seconds

Cat Whitehill uses her body and a little slight of hand to hold off the Swedish forward until goalie Hope Solo wins the ball.

1...2...

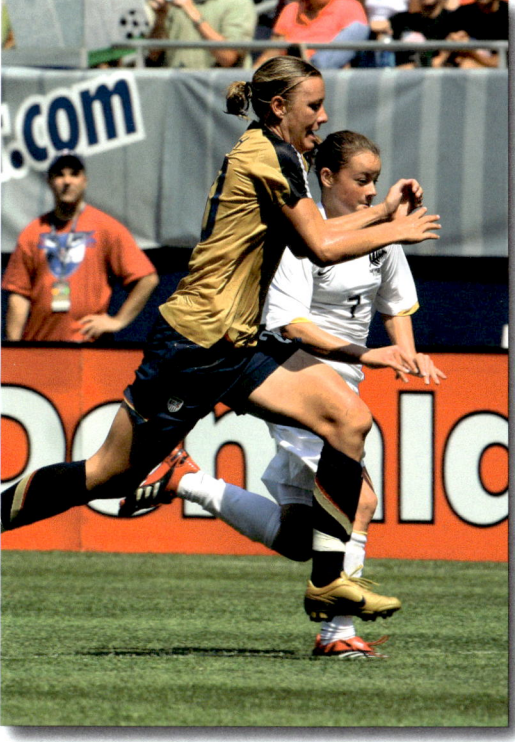

Three Seconds of Domination

Abby Wambach uses her size, strength and speed to clear out a New Zealand defender.

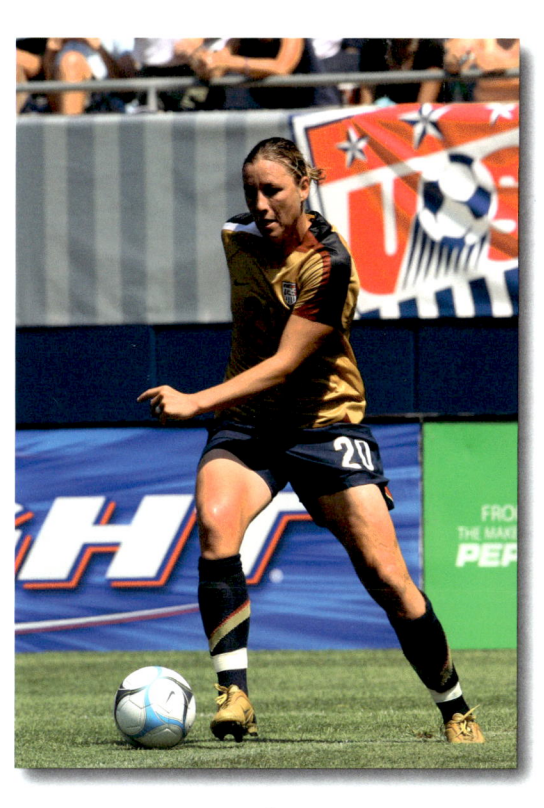

143

Three Seconds to Calculate

Kristine Lilly searches the field to see where other players are as she chases down a loose ball against North Korea.

3

4

...3

7

Photo vest worn by
Paul Phillips on the sidelines
during the World Cup games; later
autographed by the players.

145

146

Portrait

OF PASSION

Published by Competitive Image Publishing, Inc.
PO Box 19174
Minneapolis, MN 55419
telephone 612 578 0669
email **portraitinfo@portraitofpassion.com**
website **portraitofpassion.com**

First Paperback edition, 2008

©2008 Competitive Image Publishing Inc.
Photographs ©2007 Paul H. Phillips
Text ©2008 Gail B. Stewart
Foreword ©2008 Julie Foudy

All rights reserved. No part of this book may be reproduced in any manner in any media or transmitted by any means whatsoever, electronic or mechanical (including photocopy, film or video recording, Internet posting, or any other information storage and retrieval system) without the the prior written permission of the publisher.

LIBRARY OF CONGRESS CATALOGING-IN-PUBLICATION DATA

Stewart, Gail B. (Gail Barbara), 1949–

Portrait of Passion / written by Gail B. Stewart ; photographed by Paul H. Phillips ; foreword by Julie Foudy.

p. ; cm.

ISBN 978-0-9801948-0-7

1. Women soccer players—United States—Biography. 2. Soccer teams—United States—Pictorial works. 3. Soccer for women—United States. I. Title. II. Phillips, Paul H. III. Foudy, Julie, 1971–

GV944.5 S74 2008
796.334'082—dc22
2008920689

Printed by The John Roberts Company, Minneapolis
Printed and bound in the United States of America
Designed by Carl Franzén

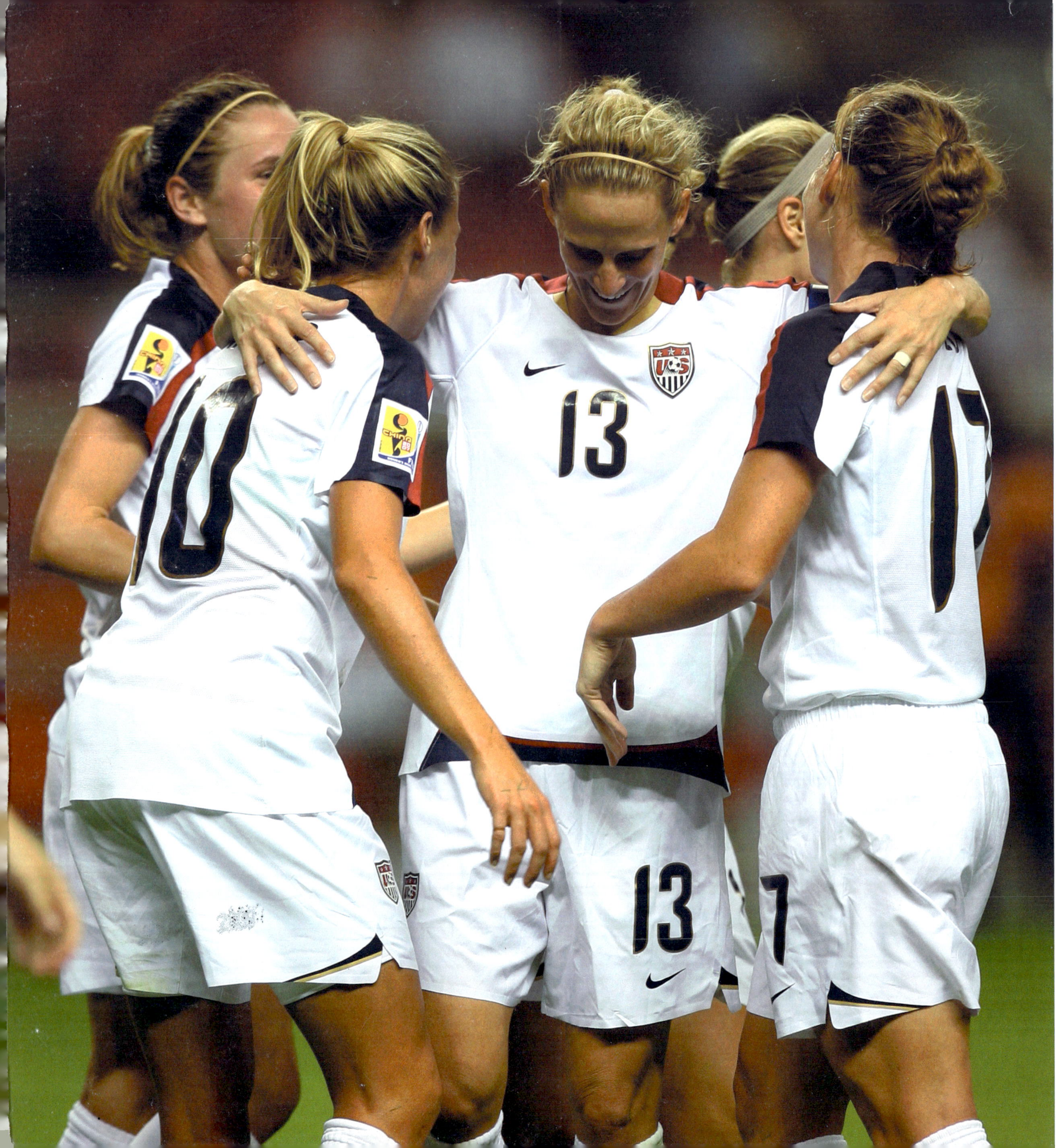
10
13
13